Richard F. Burton

Twayne's English Authors Series

Herbert Sussman, Editor

Northeastern University

TEAS 412

SIR RICHARD FRANCIS BURTON
(1821–1890)
Portrait by Lord Leighton, 1876
Photograph courtesy of the
National Portrait Gallery, London

Richard F. Burton

By Glenn S. Burne

University of North Carolina at Charlotte

Twayne Publishers • Boston

Richard F. Burton

Glenn S. Burne

Copyright © 1985 by G.K. Hall & Company
All Rights Reserved
Published by Twayne Publishers
A Division of G.K. Hall & Company
70 Lincoln Street
Boston, Massachusetts 02111

Book Production by Elizabeth Todesco
Book Design by Barbara Anderson

Printed on permanent/durable acid-free
paper and bound in the United States of
America.

Library of Congress Cataloging in Publication Data

Burne, Glenn S. (Glenn Stephen), 1921–
    Richard F. Burton.

    (Twayne's English authors series; TEAS 412)
    Bibliography: p. 158
    Includes index.
    1. Burton, Richard Francis, Sir, 1821–1890.
2. Authors, English—19th century—Biography.
3. Scholars—Great Britain—Biography.
4. Explorers—Great Britain—Biography.
I. Title. II. Series.
PR4349.B52Z59   1985   808'.0092'4[B]   85-8586
ISBN 0-8057-6903-X

For Anita

Contents

About the Author

After graduating from the University of California at Berkeley, Glenn S. Burne studied in France for two years and subsequently received his doctorate in comparative literature from the University of Washington. His publications include a book on Remy de Gourmont, a volume of translations of Gourmont, and a book on Julian Green, along with articles and reviews on modern French and American literature. Professor Burne teaches modern literature at the University of North Carolina at Charlotte, where he served as chairman of the English Department from 1971 to 1977. He is a member of the Southern Comparative Literature Association, the Modern Language Association, and is past president of the Philological Association of the Carolinas.

Preface

Every historical age produces a handful of men and women who stand so far outside their societies, whose personalities and careers are so brilliant and bizarre and their achievements so great, that we can rarely account for them—we can only stand in awe of them, admire their works, and wonder at the enormous gulf that separates them from ordinary people. Such a man was Sir Richard Francis Burton. His accomplishments were enormous, and yet, in the opinion of some recent scholars, the man was even greater than his works—an opinion shared by others who had the rare fortune to know him personally. Burton is remembered today principally as one of the intrepid explorers of the Near East and Africa who was involved in the discovery of the source of the Nile, and as the (equally intrepid) translator of an unexpurgated version of *The Arabian Nights.* During his life (1821–90) he traveled so widely, explored so deeply into unknown and usually hostile lands, that one can only marvel at his prodigious literary production. He published forty-three volumes of explorations and travel, two volumes of poetry, over 100 articles, six volumes of translated Portuguese literature, two volumes of translated Latin poetry, four volumes of folklore—Neapolitan, African, and Hindu, all with extensive annotations—and the sixteen-volume translation of *The Arabian Nights,* also with annotations and lengthy commentary. He also left a mass of journals and diaries, most of which were burned by his wife after his death. Fortunately, a number of manuscripts survived, along with numerous personal letters.

"Discovery is mostly my mania," Burton very accurately said of himself, but his real passion was not so much for geographical discovery as it was for "the hidden in man, for the unknowable, and inevitably the unthinkable."[1] Indeed, his driving curiosity, his obsession to know, led him to explore those aspects of human life which most of his contemporaries considered dirty, unhealthy, morbid, obscene, and demonic. He was often condemned, and was admired mainly for his more obvious exploits of territorial discovery. He was a precursor of Freud and Havelock Ellis in his preoccupations and insights, and because of the sexual nature of much of his writing, he was obliged to have many of his works privately printed. The Society for the Suppression of Vice was very active in Burton's day and caused numerous authors and publishers to be prosecuted for their "immoral" works, such as the seventy-year-old Henry Vizetelly, who, in 1888, was fined and sentenced to three months in prison for publishing Havelock Ellis's translation of Zola's *La Terre*. Vizetelly died a disgraced and ruined man.[2]

Burton can be included in the front rank of three classes of gifted men. First, he is in the company of the great nineteenth-century explorers like David Livingstone, Henry Morton Stanley, John Hanning Speke, and Samuel Baker, all of whom followed in the African footsteps of the earlier Mungo Park and James Bruce; he also ranks among those brilliant and often amateur scientists—Charles Darwin, Francis Galton, Charles Lyell, James G. Frazer, A. H. Sayce, Thomas Huxley, and Havelock Ellis—all enthusiastic explorers of the unknown; and third, Burton was a literary man, a poet and translator, and one of the nineteenth century's foremost linguists. Perhaps the best concise account of Sir Richard appeared in an obituary by J. S. Cannon in 1890: "He was fond of calling himself an anthropologist, by which he meant that he took for his domain everything that concerns man and woman. Whatever humanity does he refused to consider common or unclean; and he dared to write down in black and white (for private circulation) the results of his exceptional experience. . . . His virility is stamped on everything he said or wrote. . . . He concealed nothing; he boasted of nothing. . . . But to those who were admitted to his intimacy, the man was greater than what he did or what he wrote."[3] That the man was greater than what he wrote may be true. It seems to be the consensus of his many biographers who have recounted, some in sensational "exposés," some with responsible scholarship, Burton's truly remarkable life. But there is no question that Burton was also a writer of lasting importance whose many books of travel and exploration made a valuable contribution to modern knowledge of geography and anthropology, just as his translations contributed richly to modern literature.

This book is primarily concerned with Burton as a writer; but in dealing with him as a man of letters, we will be inescapably involved with his life, since his travel books, whatever else they are about, are about Burton. He is a strong presence in all his narratives; his anthropology is always intermixed with autobiography.

We will consider Burton's publications in more or less chronological order, as he moves through various stages of his writing career. He wrote many books, probably too many, so that some will be merely mentioned in passing. His major achievements will be studied in detail, and in each case we will comment on form, style, and substance; we will identify and evaluate the distinctive features of the work—those features which provide its unique qualities as a work of literature.

Glenn S. Burne

University of North Carolina at Charlotte

Acknowledgments

The photograph of a portrait of Richard Burton by Sir Frederick Leighton (1876) is provided courtesy of the National Portrait Gallery, London.

I wish to thank Anita Moss for her support and encouragement, and the College of Arts and Sciences of the University of North Carolina at Charlotte, for providing me with a semester free of teaching duties in order that I might work on this project.

Chronology

1859   Returns to England and engages in bitter public controversy with Speke over the true source of the Nile River.

1860   *Lake Regions of Central Africa*. Travels across America to Rocky Mountains, Salt Lake City, and on to the Pacific coast.

1861   Returns to England. 22 January marries Isabel Arundell. *The City of the Saints*.

1861–1863   Consul in Foreign Service, assigned to island of Fernando Po. Explores territories in west Africa.

1863–1864   Mission to visit the king of Dahomy.

1864   *A Mission to Gelele, King of Dahome*.

1864–1869   Consul in Brazil. Explores hinterland.

1865   *Wit and Wisdom from West Africa*.

1869   *The Highlands of Brazil*.

1869–1871   Consul in Damascus, Syria.

1870   *Vikram and the Vampire* and *Letters from the Battlefields of Paraguay*.

1871   *Unexplored Syria*.

1871–1872   Returns for a year's stay in England.

1872   *Zanzibar*.

1872–1875   Stationed in Trieste.

1875   *Ultima Thule*.

1875–1876   Revisits India with wife Isabel.

1876   *Etruscan Bologna* and *Two Trips to Gorilla Land*.

1876–1880   Explores Midian in search of gold.

1877   *Sind Revisited*.

1878   *The Gold Mines of Midian*.

1879   *The Land of Midian (Revisited)*.

1880   *The Kasidah of Haji Abdu El-Yezdi* and *Os Lusiads (The Lusiads)*.

1880–1885   Travels to Egypt and Morocco.

1881   *Camoens: His Life and his Lusiads*.

1881–1882   Explores the Gold Coast of West Africa.

Chapter One

Burton's Life:
Quest and Controversy

Richard Burton was, to say the least, controversial, and he could be a most difficult man personally. In appearance he was formidable: about six feet tall, muscular and agile, and with a dark, intense, brooding face that reminded people of the devil, or what they thought the devil would look like. Arthur Symons said Burton's visage seems to have conjured up thoughts of Satan; Swinburne said he had "the jaw of a devil and the brow of a god"; and the earl of Dunraven wrote that Burton "prided himself on looking like Satan— as indeed he did."[1] Burton apparently even contemplated writing "a biography of Satan himself," but actually he was preoccupied, as we have seen, with an incredible number of other things.

His manner as well as his appearance was found to be disturbing by many observers. On social occasions he would scowl, bristle, and make remarks designed to shock or astonish: "he would throw out his quills like a porcupine" and make observations that earned him the title of the "infamous Captain Burton."[2] He was an accomplished street fighter and playground brawler in his boyhood and was an equally formidable opponent with words (or, if he could get any takers, with the sword) in his maturity. He engaged in verbal duels with the editors and publishers who rejected or denounced his writings and actions, retaliating in spirited fashion to charges of indecency, filth, and pornography which were often directed at him and his books. About the character of his wife, Isabel Arundell Burton, biographers are divided, as they are about whether the marriage was a success or a disaster, whether she was an admirable woman or "answerable for most of Burton's troubles."[3] Of one thing we are certain: she was greatly troubled by her husband's preoccupation with the erotic in life and literature. She urged him frequently to abandon his researches, his translations of such Eastern erotica as *The Scented Garden,* and she wasted no time after his death in getting rid of many of his "objectionable" papers. She then set about writing

1

the biography of "the most pure, the most refined, the most modest
man . . . who ever lived."[4] It is to her sometimes unreliable rec-
ollections of Burton that modern biographers are obliged to turn.

The Early Years: Wanderings in Europe

Richard Francis Burton was born of mixed Irish and Scottish
parents at Torquay, England, on 21 March 1821. He was taken to
France before he was a year old, but returned with his parents for
long visits. He had a sister and a younger brother, Edward, with
whom he shared many boyhood escapades. He had slight regard for
his father, who had resigned his commission as a lieutenant-colonel
in the British Army, preferring to live a leisurely life in Europe
supported by his wife's inherited income; and he seems to have had
mixed feelings about his mother. He rarely mentions either in his
writings and apparently felt bitter toward his mother for her mis-
managing an inheritance he might have received. He "felt cheated,
deprived, unsure of affection," and late in life observed sourly that
a man is mostly what his mother makes of him. He was in no hurry
to marry, remaining single until he was almost forty—seven years
after the death of his mother.[5]

None of the family cared for England. The children were enrolled
for a time in English schools, but the family moved back to France
at the earliest opportunity—which came in the form of a measles
epidemic at the boys' school. They returned to the place which
Burton was always to look back on most fondly, Beauséjour, a small
chateau in Tours. They settled in with the English colony of some
200 English families, and Burton's father, an indolent man but an
avid hunter, never worked again, preferring to live off his wife's
small inheritance. Beauséjour was a romantic spot situated on the
river Loire, with a garden, vineyards, a fine view, hunting, and
picnicking, and with several nearby castles to feed the youthful
imagination. In fact, the young Richard liked to fancy he was
descended from French royalty. During these early years he received
a haphazard formal education, but did develop interests and talents
which would serve him well in later years. When he was nine the
family left Tours for a life of incessant wandering—fourteen moves
in ten years. This nomadic existence was upsetting to the young
boy (though it was to become the pattern of his mature life), but
he made the most of it, learning several languages along with nu-

merous regional dialects and becoming quite the young cosmopolite. Later Burton wrote, "In consequence of being brought up abroad, we never thoroughly understood English society, nor did society understand us. . . . England is the only country where I never felt at home." Burton did not, however, emerge from his many years in France as a Frenchman (he expressed his regret at not being born French); instead he grew up ambivalent about both nations, lacking any strong sense of national identity, counting himself, in his words, "a waif, a stray . . . a blaze of light without a focus."[6] He was to become the inveterate wanderer.

The father dragged his family to various places in France and then to Italy: Lyon, then Livorno, Pisa, Siena, Rome, and finally Naples, with Richard precociously picking up local languages and dialects along the way. He also became accomplished in swimming, dancing, shooting, lovemaking (at least as it was taught by Italian medical students he came to know), and, above all, in swordsmanship. An enthusiastic and accomplished fencer, he combined French and Neapolitan techniques; he became a master, and many years later he wrote a military instructional manual on the subject and even gathered hundreds of manuscript pages for a sociohistoric study of the sword's symbolic and cultural significance, *The Book of the Sword,* which he did not publish until late in life, in 1884.

Concerned about his sons' education, Burton's father assigned a tutor, an ineffective Englishman, whom the boys detested, to look after the boys' development. The young Richard successfully resisted most of what the tutor had to offer, but he did emerge from those nomadic years with a firsthand cosmopolitan education in European art and architecture, geography, an intimate familiarity with varieties of social behavior in different regions of France and Italy, and a sexual sophistication far beyond what most boys of his age would have had. And although his attentions were considerably dispersed, he was gradually acquiring a focus to his interests. He had developed a passion for languages and was on his way to achieving mastery of several—French at Tours, Bearnais (a mixture of French, Spanish, and Provençal) at Pau, Italian in northern Italy, a bit of spoken Greek at Marseilles, and Neapolitan dialect in Naples (which enabled him in later years to make the first English translation, published posthumously in 1893, of Giovanni Battista Basile's *Il Pentamerone,* a collection of Neapolitan folktales that some consider to rival those of Boccaccio). Eventually Burton learned Spanish and some German, and became sufficiently proficient in Portuguese to translate Ca-moens's *Lusiads* (1880).

These were more than just intellectual achievements; they enabled him to get close to the people wherever he lived, to be accepted by them, to be able to study them. Burton radiated an interest and curiosity about local culture and was rewarded by an unusually friendly reception. He took as his motto *"Omne solum forti patria,"* which he translated as "For every region is a strong man's home."

While in Naples, Burton engaged, at the age of fifteen, in numerous love affairs, escapades with prostitutes, derring-do on the lava-covered slopes of Vesuvius, and acts of bravery—or bravado—during an outbreak of cholera, when he and his younger brother disguised themselves in undertakers' garb and traveled about the city, at night, helping gather corpses for mass burials. "A courageous and macabre adventure, worthy of Burton in Mecca and Burton in Africa," and he told of it years later with a "grave relish."[7]

After a winter in Pisa, however—what with the Burton boys consorting with the sexually active Italian medical students and experimenting with alcohol and opium, fighting and carousing in the streets, bringing trouble with the police—the father decided to send the boys back to school in England. Richard wanted to go to college in Toulouse but father was adamant—England it would be, Oxford for Richard and Cambridge for Edward, with careers as clergymen, of all things, for both.

The Oxford Misadventures

So, back to the "chill and dolorous north" where they renewed their violent distaste for everything English. Burton's career at Oxford was characteristically turbulent.[8] He had trouble, at first, in accepting traditional hazing, even challenging an upperclassman to a duel, Heidelberg style. It never came off, and Burton, after more than his share of fist fights, was accepted into the company of his fellow students, largely because he showed himself to be a good sport, even more because they respected his courage and honesty, his imposing physique, his abilities as a fighter, and his bizarre brilliance—which was rarely focused in designated areas and gave scant promise of his later success. Indeed, failure was to be his experience at Oxford. He did meet and have discussions with some of the notable men of the day—John Henry Newman, Thomas

Arnold, and Benjamin Jowett—and he made friends with the local fencing master, but he could not resist practical jokes and other pranks which eventually got him expelled; however, not until he tried, at his father's insistence, for a fellowship. He was rejected, apparently, not because of his scholarly defects but because of his superiority in knowledge and talent. His mastery of both classical and modern Greek—the vernacular spoken by merchants in Marseilles—offended, or at least was not recognized by, his conservative examiners, and he was failed—for "gross errors of pronunciation." He also refused to imitate Anglicized Latin—he conversed instead in "Roman Latin" and was ridiculed by his professors. Honors went to the mediocrities who properly aped the local dons, and Burton retired in contempt.

One fortunate consequence: Burton was inspired to show the Oxford masters—to show them up—so he did not abandon languages but shifted to an exotic one—Arabic, which turned out to be his most useful personal and literary tongue. He sought out tutors, and also developed a strong talent for studying on his own. He made rapid progress, vowing to become the greatest linguist of his time.

Burton deliberately tried to get himself "rusticated" (a temporary suspension) from Oxford. He indulged in a series of pranks, such as circulating caricatures of the university officials, and throwing wild wine parties; but he received only a reprimand. Finally, he induced several of his fellows to absent themselves from a lecture and to attend a steeple-chase, in direct defiance of a college order. His fellow culprits were awarded temporary suspensions; Burton was expelled. He carried off his disgrace as well as possible, consoled by the fact that his brother Edward had similarly managed an expulsion from Cambridge. (Edward was later to become a medical doctor.)

Passage to India

Meanwhile, during Burton's misadventures at Oxford, certain events were occurring in India that were to have a decisive effect on Burton's life and professional career. The British Empire, largely in the form of the British East India Company, was extending and solidifying its control in India and neighboring countries. England's power seemed to be beyond question until in January of 1842 a bloody uprising and massacre took place in Afghanistan, and the British troops, along with thousands of civilians, fled south into India. This aroused a new interest in strengthening the British position in India, an interest that was shared by Burton. This fact, along with Burton's recent expulsion from Oxford, resulted in his resolve to go east. Father agreed, and a commission was purchased for him in the "Bombay Army," a military organization created and administered by the commercial British East India Company.

When Burton arrived in India in October 1842, he was decidedly unimpressed by the exotic East, as represented by squalid Bombay, but he nevertheless threw himself enthusiastically into the study of the most widespread of the Hindi dialects—Hindustani. He found local teachers, and despite his dismay at the filth and chaos of local life, he soon mastered the language along with local customs, beliefs, and practices. Far from holding himself aloof from the local Indians, Burton learned to pass as one of them and thereby gained admission into native society.[9] He also studied both Sanskrit and Gujarti, which was the language of the Parsees, and eventually went on to master Persian, Sindi, Punjabi, Teluga, Pashto, Multani, Armenian, and Turkish. In addition, he took a scholarly interest in Asian cultures, collecting books and befriending English scholars and Orientalists living in India. He became so sincerely involved in native culture that his fellow officers called him "white nigger." This did not bother Burton in the least: he persevered, especially with the study of Arabic, which remained his favorite language, and he often wrote describing its lyrical, mystical, and aesthetic qualities.[10] Eventually, he reached his goal as one of the leading linguists of his time, mastering in the end twenty-nine languages and about forty dialects.

While in India Burton learned not only the many languages but everything he could about Indian culture. He sampled everything "with great gusto—the conventional and the unconventional, the respectable and the tabooed."[11] Without his mastery of languages he could never have gained access to his many adventures. He even tried alligator wrestling and snake-charming, learned the Sepoy wrestling techniques and their horsemanship, which he considered superior to that of the British, and in exchange he taught his improved brand of swordsmanship to the native troops under his command.

By and large Burton was bored by British colonial society and sought out experiences among the Indians, engaging apparently in several love affairs, one of which, with a beautiful Persian girl, he seemed never to have gotten over. He wrote lyrical love poems to and about this unknown young woman, and a moving elegy on the occasion of her premature death. Ever after he had a special affection for the Persians, whom he considered to be a "gifted race," beautiful physically and possessing "the richest and most charming of Eastern languages."

An important development in Burton's life was his becoming a translator and intelligence agent under Sir Charles Napier, commandant of the Bombay Army in northern India. This fierce Scotsman had defeated thousands of native troops and brought under British control hundreds of local chiefs, along with over 50,000 square miles of the area in northern India known as Sind (variously spelled Sindh and Scinde). Burton was active in Napier's efforts to bring peace to the region, to eliminate brigandage, exploitative taxation, barbarous laws, and savage punishments, and to introduce a higher standard of living by way of improved agricultural techniques. In remote villages Burton did everything from infiltrating native society to performing routine translations at court trials. He continued to study languages and local dialects and to observe the operations of European archeologists in the area, whom he ridiculed at first—he even planted fake artifacts (but later, when among the Etruscan ruins in Italy, he was to become a respected practitioner of the new science).

During this time Burton broke with English precedent in learning to disguise himself successfully as an Indian, instead of relying on the usual paid informers. He would stain his face with walnut juice, wear false beards and elaborate native clothing, and enter native society as a wealthy merchant. Justifying his slight accent by purporting to be from some remote province of the Moslem world, he would sit conversing for hours in the native bazaars or would invite himself to Indian social functions, thereby acquiring an enormous amount of firsthand information about native attitudes and practices. He was able to see the Englishman as the Indian sees him, to get a deep insight into Indian life and culture.

There was more to Burton's disguises and masquerades, however, than mere intelligence work—he was in a sense acting out his own fantasies: "the elaborate pretense took courage and acting talent, of which he had an abundance, as well as a thirst for the forbidden, which had been with him since childhood." So he was a tremendous success as Mirza Abdullah, merchant. He said he "secured numberless invitations, was proposed to by several papas, and won, or had to think he won, a few hearts."[12]

But not all of Burton's activities were an unqualified success. There occurred in 1845 one event of decisive importance that had a long-term effect on both his life and career. His chief, Sir Charles Napier, asked Burton to look into a native practice for which Sir Charles had a total abhorrence: the open pursuit of homosexuality, which, in Sind, was tolerated to a far greater extent than in other Moslem regions. Napier, deeply disturbed by rumors that certain homosexual brothels in Karachi were attracting and corrupting his troops, requested Burton to investigate and write a report. The report was detailed and explicit, as Burton always was, and when it came to the attention of certain high-ranking officers who had no affection for Burton, they used it to discredit his personal morality, suggesting strongly that in his case there was no difference between objective observation and personal participation. He could not be formally punished for following orders in writing his report, but his typical honesty was used against him, making his continued stay in India an impossibility, and creating an ugly shadow that hung over him for years after he left India. He departed Sind in May 1849, a sick man emotionally and physically, since in addition to his other troubles, he suffered from cholera and ophthalmia.

Burton Considers Marriage

Back in England the dark rumors resulted in his being shunned and suspect—even though he wrote thousands of words on the attractiveness of Oriental women and of his many love affairs. He did not write on the subject of pederasty, however, either publicly or privately, until 1884, when he included a courageous essay on the subject (doubtless drawing on his investigations at Karachi) in the "Terminal Essay" of *The Arabian Nights.*

Perhaps a side effect of this experience was that when Burton came back from India at age twenty-nine he was convinced that he should get married. Indeed, he spent about four years in a more or less earnest quest to marry a "virtuous woman." So despite his reputation, he had a number of love affairs, the young ladies tending to be much enchanted by his dark, brooding good looks, his man-of-the-world demeanor, and possibly by the legends of his exotic past. Parents, however, saw him as totally unsuitable, feeling that his future was as questionable as his past, and they threw effective roadblocks in his path.

For Isabel Arundel, however, who was to become Mrs. Burton, the roadblocks were only temporarily effective. She writes eloquently of his impact on her romantic sensibility, her conviction that he would some day be her husband, and her determination, after meeting him, to wait him out. She was an attractive young lady who felt that because of her hardy nature and love for romance and adventure, she would be the perfect mate for the unconventional and restless Burton. [13] She was going to have to wait for a long time, however, as Burton chafed under the restrictions and routine of European life "amongst mothers and sisters"—"four years' life of European effeminacy" and his memories, evidently, of the "soft, bending, and relaxed" Oriental women he had known. [14]

First Books on India

So, during his years from age twenty-nine to thirty-two he did not succeed in getting married, but he did work energetically on his writing. His health gradually returned, along with his ambitions, and he turned out four large books on India in the years 1851 and 1852. *Goa and the Blue Mountains* was an account of the varied inhabitants of Goa, the Hindus of Malabar, and the mountain-dwelling Todas who practiced polygamy. This was followed immediately by *Scinde; or the Unhappy Valley,* a narrative of his travels through northern Sind with a friend, Captain Walter Scott of the Bombay Engineers. The third book, *Sindh, and the Races that Inhabit the Valley of the Indus,* was a first-rate ethnological study; and the fourth, *Falconry in the Valley of the Indus,* was a short book on hunting, but it also contained some ethnological data and useful autobiographical material. But for all their merits, none of these books was especially successful. Burton was bitter over the popular failure of his Indian writings—as well as the failure of his love affairs—and he in 1852 turned to writing a very different kind of book: *A Complete System of Bayonet Exercise,* a thirty-six-page pamphlet designed to improve the British infantryman's capacity for killing people. It brought him negative criticism in England but was well received abroad, especially in Germany.

Arabian Pilgrimage

Before the publication of *Bayonet Exercise* Burton had once again taken up a scheme he had devised while still in India: penetration and exploration of the "forbidden" city of Mecca. The penalty for entry into the sacred city—at least if one were caught at it—was certain death. A few Europeans had successfully gained entrance to the ancient city, but only John L. Burkhardt, a notable Swiss Arabist, had described it in any detail. Burton, always attracted by the forbidden and dangerous, resolved to penetrate both Mecca and the equally sacred Medina and to write about them firsthand: "Thoroughly tired of 'progress' and of 'civilization,' curious to see with my own eyes what others are content to 'hear with their ears,' namely, Moslem inner life in a really Mohammedan country; and longing, if truth be told, to set foot on that mysterious spot which no vacation tourist has yet described, measured, sketched, and photographed, I resolved to resume my old character of a Persian wanderer, a 'Darwaysh,' and to make the attempt."[15]

So in autumn of 1852, Burton was in London with a detailed plan in hand, to try to gain permission and financial backing. He met with enthusiastic support from several members of the Royal Geographical Society; those who had valued Burton's India books found the Mecca idea both plausible and exciting, and with their support he gained a leave of absence from the East India Company. He planned, in addition to penetrating Mecca and Medina, to explore east of Mecca, to cross the Arabian peninsula, and to fill in the great blank spaces that stood for Arabia on British maps. Accordingly, he refurbished his Arabic and reviewed the complex details of Moslem behavior and etiquette, in order to "so recondition his reflexes that he moved, thought, ate, and performed all bodily functions as an Arab rather than as a 'Frank' [the Middle Eastern name for the white Europeans]."[16]

After spending some months in Egypt perfecting his new role as an Arab "doctor," Burton began his pilgrimage to Mecca. With a long beard descending from a shaven head, his skin stained with walnut juice, and garbed in flowing robes, he was once again Mirza Abdullah, and thus disguised successfully to deceive his way into the sacred cities. His appearance, manners, and practices were apparently perfect, and he again explained his slight accent by claiming to be a Pathan, an Indian of Afghan parentage. He traveled south from Suez on the overcrowded pilgrim ship, jammed to the gunwales with devotees of Allah, experiencing all the privations of his fellow Moslems. The trip across the deserts to Medina and Mecca was perhaps even more dangerous than the actual penetration of the sacred cities. Burton had joined a small caravan that was repeatedly attacked by Bedouin bandits, and a number of natives and camels were killed. He had with him two Arab servants who tried to look after him; they took care of his meager baggage, fended off beggars, and cooked for him his standard meals of boiled rice, fried locusts, rancid butter, fried onions, and date paste. He took what notes he could, surreptitiously, in a microscopic script, since notetaking was not only forbidden, once inside the city, but would arouse suspicion in any situation. He had to write most of his notes at night, in the seclusion and darkness of his own tent or room. He spent a month at Medina in the home of a sheikh who had accepted him at face value, whence he ventured forth to visit various shrines, most important of which was the burial place of Fatimah, Mohammed's favorite daughter.

Burton then joined a caravan for Mecca and spent many days of acute discomfort traversing the sun-baked, hostile terrain. Dead animals, and occasionally dead people, strewed the route, and several travelers were shot down in ambushes by the local bandits. They traveled mostly at night, to escape the hazards of the day, and entered the holy city by night. On his arrival Burton stayed in the home of one of his servants, who had been raised in Mecca, and on the first morning he set out to see the sights—the Great Mosque and the sacred Kaaba, "navel of the world" set in "the mother of cities." Burton participated in all the ritual observances while secretly measuring and noting the holy artifacts. He also made the required visit to Mount Arafat (not to be confused with Ararat), where Gabriel was said to have instructed Adam in prayer, and he even penetrated into the holiest of shrines, the "great cube" of the Kaaba itself.

All went well; he passed every scrutiny undetected, though well aware that if caught he might not get as far as official justice but would be cut down by the nearest true believer. At times he felt under surveillance but nothing came of it. He had mingled with every type of Moslem and had gathered all the information he wanted about both the people and their many shrines, and he was ready to depart. Six precarious days had provided a wealth of material, and, deciding to forego the projected trip east across the Arabian desert (he had been assured by all he questioned that it would be foolish and no doubt fatal), he headed back to the Red Sea.

Feeling elated by his success, Burton remained in Arab disguise, spending the remaining weeks of his leave of absence in Cairo, writing up his account of his experiences. Then, rather than returning to England, he sailed to Bombay, where he finished the book, *A Pilgrimage to Meccah and Al-Medinah* (1855–56). He then turned his attentions to his next venture into the forbidden and unknown: the penetration of Harar, the religious capital of Somaliland, "citadel of Moslem learning and missionary activity, and center of East African slave trade."[17]

First African Aventures

For this adventure, Burton teamed up with John Hanning Speke, a young officer in the Bengal Native Infantry, who was to figure importantly in Burton's later search for the source of the Nile, and two other officers from the East India service. He assigned his three associates to various investigations in Somaliland—explorations of the interior and the gathering of information on the slave trade—but he reserved the city of Harar for himself. He had decided to forego his usual native disguise and to travel openly as an Englishman on "special mission" to open relations with the amir of Harar. In this he was successful: he entered the city in 1854, was well received, and managed to gather copious notes on Somali Bedouin life, including their bizarre sexual customs, which he was later to write up in his *First Footsteps in East Africa* (1856), along with a vocabulary of special Harari words included in an appendix.

It was later to become apparent that the city of Harar was not Burton's principal objective. While there he spent considerable time and effort in gathering information about his real interest—the mystery of the source of the Nile—and so in 1855 he planned a second Somali expedition. He had studied the various legends and semimythical accounts of the unknown source, especially the records of James Bruce, who, in 1768–70, had found the source of the Blue Nile, a tributary of the main river, the White Nile. Bruce had left a body of geographical observations that were not always credited by British geographers but had considerable influence on Burton's theories. So, in 1855, Burton set out from Zanzibar, the island close to the east coast of Africa, with a small group, including John Speke, to see what he could find. They were attacked by natives, and while Burton and Speke managed to escape with their lives, one of the young officers was killed. Burton and Speke were both severely wounded—Burton with a spear through his cheek and jaw—and the expedition was abandoned. Thus these "first footsteps" were less than successful, but they did bring attention to the flourishing slave trade. In fact, the British authorities used the death of the young officer as an excuse to destroy much of that widespread trade.[18]

England and Isabel Again

Burton's *Pilgrimage* was well received, and the author was invited to speak on his adventures in Arabia and Harar before the Royal Geographical Society in June of 1855. But at that time the African exploits were being overshadowed by the Crimean War, and Burton, and other officers from the British East India Company, requested and were granted extended leaves to participate in the Crimea, where they were generally badly treated because of the regular army officers' hostility to those from the British East India Company. However, Burton was made chief of staff of a small contingent of Moslem Turks, under the command of another officer from India. In this position Burton found his knowledge of Turkish, horsemanship, and saber drill to be highly useful, but he also found the entire experience in the Crimea to be appallingly bad. He was disgusted by the general lack of discipline and the poor leadership, which, in his opinion, resulted in incredible losses of British troops and supplies. Burton wrote virtually nothing about that war experience. To him it was a mere unpleasant interlude between explorations, and he got out of the war as soon as possible.[19]

Back in England Burton met Isabel Arundel once again and the relationship flourished to the point where he actually proposed marriage—warning Isabel of the kind of life she would have to lead, cut off from England, friends, and family.[20] But Isabel, young, romantic, and very much in love, was delighted, and they became informally engaged. That is, her father approved, but the mother was adamantly opposed to the union. However, Burton left again for Africa before anything was formally announced, let alone consummated. Actually, both were willing to delay the announcement—the "idea" was perhaps more appealing than the fact. This was to become the pattern of their lives—Richard continually taking off for parts unknown, usually without Isabel.

Into Central Africa

Once again Burton teamed up with John Speke for the new expedition into the interior of Africa, sailing from Bombay and arriving in Zanzibar in December 1856. They were warned against the projected venture by the British Resident in Zanzibar, who had spent fifteen years in the area. Undaunted, they proceeded to prepare for an elaborate expedition which was to last two years. Their departure was delayed for six months, however, due to red tape and the failure of the third member to arrive—Dr. John Steinhaeuser, an old friend of Burton's from India, who had become ill. The time was spent in preliminary explorations along the coast, and by Burton taking voluminous notes toward his book on Zanzibar, in which he documented the unrelieved horror of the place. Filth, disease, stench, decay, and a demoralized native population were the main characteristics of the island, as well as being the center of the slave trade. To Burton conditions in Zanzibar were worse than anything he had seen in India.

The expedition into the interior of Africa finally got underway on 16 June 1857. It lasted twenty-one months, during which time Burton and Speke experienced every conceivable hardship of mind and body, a journey that saw the relationship between the two men turn from friendship to rivalry to bitter mutual hatred and ultimately to tragedy. The party moved inland in a generally westward direction from the coast toward the lake regions of central Africa. The trip went badly from the beginning—the extensive equipment and supplies were soon lost along the way, by natural disaster or theft by numerous deserters. Diseases took their toll and life was turned into a hell by the ravages of carnivorous insects. Nevertheless, the explorers finally arrived on the shores of the great inland sea, which turned out to be Lake Tanganyika, the longest and one of the deepest fresh-water lakes in the world. They set up camp at a small town on the shore, from which they explored the lake and surrounding country, hoping to find the outlet that would prove to be the beginnings of the Nile. Both Burton and Speke were sick much of the time, Speke nearly blind from inflammation of the eyes, Burton suffering from a paralysis of the legs.

Speke, when his eyes improved, suggested a trip to the north, to another great body of water they had heard about. Burton, making one of the major mistakes of his life, rejected the idea and sent Speke on alone—to discover Lake Victoria Nyanza, which Speke correctly guessed was the headwaters of the Nile. He returned to Burton's camp jubilant over his discovery, but Burton was coldly skeptical, clinging to his original theory that Lake Tanganyika was the true source. Relations between the two men had been going badly, due to mutual incompatibility and jealousy. Both were hurt, Burton by his awareness that he had failed to accompany Speke on a crucial part of the trip, and Speke by Burton's refusal to admit the importance of the discovery. This would lead to continued estrangement, and while they maintained a surface cordiality and even looked after each other in later weeks, the split eventually developed into acts of betrayal, accusations, and bitter disputes when they returned to England. Speke had wanted to return to Lake Victoria to establish it definitely as the source but gave up the idea, due to lack of supplies and Burton's negative attitude, and so they returned to the coast instead.

Speke preceded Burton to England and, in spite of his promise to await Burton's arrival, made public claim to his own discovery. Burton arrived later, and a period of mutual recrimination ensued. Neither would grant much to the other, with Speke probably playing the more discreditable role. However, Speke won the day: he succeeded in gaining more money from the Royal Geographical Society to return to Africa to substantiate his claims, whereas Burton received nothing except a vote of confidence from his backers. In his book *The Lake Regions of Central Africa* (1860), Burton tried to set the record straight, according to his views, pointing out that Speke was totally dependent on him, Burton, as Speke knew nothing of the African languages, was ill informed in science and astronomy, and was unfit for anything but a subordinate role on such a demanding expedition. Burton insisted that he was responsible for the discovery of Lake Victoria even if he had not actually seen the lake with Speke, and that Speke was trying unfairly to take all the credit. Speke retaliated, giving his side of the dispute in his *What Led to the Discovery of the Source of the Nile* (1863) and *Journal of the Discovery of the Source of the Nile* (1864). Burton had his final say in the matter in his *The Nile Basin* (1864).[21]

To America and the Mormons

In the end, Speke, in the company of another explorer, James Grant, was off to Africa with a grant of £2,500, as was David Livingstone, who had recently become famous and had received £5,000 to continue his travels. Burton, a better linguist, ethnologist, and observer than all three of them, got nothing. A bitter and unhappy man, he decided to turn his attentions to a different direction, and he soon was off to Salt Lake City. He visited America in 1860, crossing the continent by stagecoach in the company of the now-recovered John Steinhaeuser from India. It was natural that Burton would take a great interest in the Mormons, especially in their custom of polygamy. The Mormons had been visited by other writers before the arrival of Burton, but "none wrote as sagacious and thorough a study as Burton."[22] He was welcomed by officials and citizens of the remote city. He was shown respect, and was invited to visit families and to inspect their homes. He read whatever he could find of their literature, and he interviewed Brigham Young. His book, *The City of the Saints* (1861), gave an essentially favorable view of Mormon life; he stressed the positive aspects of their culture and saw nothing disturbing in their form of polygamy.

In September of 1860, Burton left Salt Lake City for the Pacific coast. He had, typically, an adventurous trip, including brushes with hostile Indians, menacing wolves on the trail, and violence in Carson City, where he stayed only three days. He moved on to San Francisco where he took a boat back to England by way of Panama.

Marriage and English Social Life

Apparently Burton's experiences among the much-married Mormons did not adversely affect his own feelings about marriage, for Isabel's long wait was about to be rewarded. Despite the untiring hostility of the mother, the wedding took place in January 1861. The family was divided in its reactions, but society—that part which tended to approve the controversial Burton—was most gracious. The wedding was followed by many invitations to parties, one of the most important being that given by the socially prominent Lord Monckton Milnes, which included the presence of Lord Palmerston, then prime minister, and other notables. This led to many more parties, the publicity from which doubtless helped the sale of *Lake Regions of Central Africa* and produced numerous favorable reviews. But despite his many influential connections Burton was unable to acquire what he most desired, a consulship in one of the Arabian centers that attracted him. The best he could do was Fernando Po, a miserable, disease-ridden island off the west coast of Africa, used by the British navy for the suppression of the slave trade.

During the first several months of his marriage (before going to Fernando Po) Burton met many interesting literary people; he also joined three clubs which included notable journalists among their membership, and he spent considerable time in the company of Lord Monckton Milnes, to whose London house and country manor numerous literary celebrities were often invited. The manor, Fryston, was known as the "English mecca" for the gatherings of poets, wits, and eccentrics as well as politicians and journalists—Thomas Carlyle, Algernon Swinburne, William Thackeray, Coventry Patmore, Henry Adams, Aubry de Vere, and the Archbishop of York. Many of those whom Burton met at Fryston (but presumably not including the Archbishop) were, like Monckton Milnes himself, interested in the "peripheral areas of sexuality"—Swinburne, to be sure, and a certain Fred Hankey, who lived in Paris and collected all forms of erotica. Burton, ever the anthropologist, found Hankey to be highly interesting and even visited him in France.

At the same time, an especially close relationship developed between Burton and Swinburne, the latter then a twenty-four-year-old poet just beginning to be recognized. The brilliant and widely educated young poet was fascinated by Burton: they shared an interest in the Near East, non-Christian religions, and fine brandies. They saw each other only twice during the summer of 1861, first at a bachelor breakfast and then for a few days at Fryston, with Isabel in attendance; but later, when Burton would return to England from his consulship, they would engage in notorious drinking bouts. They remained lifelong friends and communicated frequently, and Swinburne wrote a worshipful elegiac poem on the occasion of Burton's death.

West African Adventures

Burton had been married only seven months when he was assigned to Fernando Po, but he refused to take Isabel, claiming that it was such a sinkhole of disease and depravity as to be wholly unfit for a respectable English woman—though there were many wives who did accompany their husbands to posts in West Africa. He did not return to England for eighteen months: he was evidently off on another of his many quests, and to be sure, while on Fernando Po he did not stay on the island performing his routine duties, which, at best, did not amount to much. After one week he went exploring—West African rivers, mainly the delta of the Niger, parts of southern Nigeria and the Cameroon mountains, up the Gabon River "looking for gorillas and cannibals," the lower part of the Congo River, and two trips to Dahomey, an African kingdom noted for its Amazon warriors and human sacrifices. He accumulated notes for four two-volume books totaling 2,500 pages: *Wanderings in West Africa, from Liverpool to Fernando Po* (1863); *Abeokuta and the Cameroons Mountains: An Exploration* (1863); *Two Trips to Gorilla Land and the Cataracts of the Congo* (not published until 1876); and *A Mission to Gelele, King of Dahome* (1864). He also collected native proverbs for his 450-page *Wit and Wisdom in West Africa* (1865). Thus he produced about 3,000 pages in three years, all the while, according to his own account, consuming a flask a day of brandy at Fernando Po.

The Nile Controversy

During this period Burton was surprised to find that he missed his wife, so December of 1862 found him back in London. While there (January 1863), he helped a friend named James Hunt in an important undertaking: organizing the Anthropological Society of London, which he hoped would become an organ for the publication of some of his ethnological studies that ordinary publishers either rejected or expurgated. Beginning with eleven members, the society grew into a thriving organization that included many of England's more imaginative explorers.

When Burton had left England in 1860 to go to America, John Speke and James Grant had departed for Africa, and by 1863 they had not been heard from and were long overdue. They ultimately did make it back to England after having made an historic trip of discovery, retracing the old Burton-Speke trail from Zanzibar to the lake country. They established that Lake Victoria was indeed the source of the Nile, then traveled down the river to Egypt. Just as in his turbulent relationship with Burton, Speke caused a scandal in his dealings with James Grant. He sent Grant on a side-trip while he, Speke, made the short trip to the lake and saw, alone and triumphant, the great Victoria Falls dumping into the beginning of the Nile. News of this treatment of Grant was not well received in England, nor was his public complaining about a "rescue mission" which was unavoidably delayed in its rendezvous with Speke in Egypt. In fact, the man who was the object of Speke's complaints proceeded to sue Speke for libel. At the same time Speke began to attack Burton again, stirring up a controversy which divided English geographers and explorers into two camps, with David Livingstone siding with Burton, even though he had small regard for him personally.

Burton returned from Fernando Po in August 1864, and accepted an invitation from the British Association for the Advancement of Science to debate Speke over various assertions made by both sides regarding certain aspects of geography of the lake regions of Africa. Speke, under great pressure from attacks in the press, the looming libel suit, and possible defeat by Burton in the debate, died just before the debate was to take place—"killed" presumably in a "hunting accident." Burton was sure that Speke had killed himself, but official reports called it an accident—though Speke's death from his own hunting gun was the kind that he, accomplished hunter and gun fancier, had been trained for years to avoid.[23]

This ended the debate; Burton had nothing more to say on the subject, except some sad reminiscences of the friendship between Speke and himself during their early exploring days. Many years later, especially after H. M. Stanley had traveled from Lake Tanganyika down the Congo River to the sea, Burton finally admitted that what he had discovered was the source of the Congo River.

From that time on Burton engaged in far fewer explorations. His marriage seemed to have a "taming" influence on him; he appeared to accept the conventional married life, and he made only a few minor excursions during his later years. All his great travel books were behind him by 1864. He was acknowledged as a leading explorer and ethnologist; he knew as much, perhaps more, about Africa and the Near East than anyone else around, yet he was unable to acquire what he could consider an appropriate job. No academic position was open to him, as he lacked the official "credentials," and the Foreign Office would not consider him for a diplomatic assignment or any of the consular posts that really appealed to him: Damascus, Tripoli, or Teheran. But finally he did manage to get himself transferred from Fernando Po to Santos, Brazil.

South American Adventures

Before leaving for Brazil, Burton published, without Isabel's knowledge, 200 copies of a 121-page poem called *Stone Talk,* using as a pseudonym Frank Baker, adapted from his middle name, Francis, and his mother's maiden name. The poem was bitterly satiric, attacking British "heroes" in India, British failure in the Crimea, and extolling his own militant atheism and praise for Darwin. He also had some sour things to say about marriage. On the advice of Monckton Milnes, Isabel bought up all 200 copies from various bookstores before they could come to the attention of the Foreign Office, which already had enough grievances against Burton.

Surprisingly enough, the Burtons were relatively happy in Brazil. Richard took his work seriously and kept busy with his reports and social functions. And he also found time for his writing. He began a major project that would occupy him for many years: a translation of the complete works of Portugal's leading poet, Camoens; and he also translated a volume of Hindu folktales. He published these tales in 1870 in London under the title of *Vikram and the Vampire, or Tales of Hindu Devilry.* Otherwise, life in Brazil was uneventful, but the ever-restless Burton did look around a bit in the back country and took a 1,500-mile trip down the Rio San Francisco, which resulted in another, but this time a rather dull, travel book—a "mere compilation," according to one reviewer.

In April 1868 Burton fell gravely ill, but on recovering he resigned his post in Santos and obtained permission from the Foreign Office to investigate a bloody war in which Brazil, Argentina, and Uruguay had teamed up to attack Paraguay. He visited the battlefields twice, took careful notes, and wrote a book, *Letters from the Battlefields of Paraguay,* which, published in 1870, gave the British public more accurate information and analysis than it had yet received on the subject of that war. But while Burton was wandering around in the mountains of South America word came from the

Foreign Office that he had been appointed to the cherished consulship at Damascus. Strangely enough he did not dash immediately
to London, but hung around the Paraguayan war, working on his
book—which he probably needed to reassure himself that he was
still the astute observer and effective writer of his earlier days.

Return to the Middle East

Burton went to Syria with high hopes of regaining his health and
his interest in native affairs. He succeeded in both. Syria was then
under Turkish rule, and Damascus was the scene of violent religious
hostilities. There were at least two dozen different sects of Moslems,
Jews, and Christians—all bitterly at odds with each other. In fact,
in one day in 1860 the Moslems of Damascus had slaughtered 3,000
Christians and burned their quarter of the city; but Burton characteristically plunged into native life, befriended many influential
Moslems, gave receptions which included all races and languages,
and on learning of a planned repetition of the 1860 massacre, he
organized and armed the Christians and took such precautionary
measures that the threatened attack never took place. Many Moslems
applauded Burton's actions but others were angered: nasty rumors
and accusations were spread about the Burtons, and later, when he
took steps to protect the Shazlis, an esoteric Moslem sect that had
been "secretly" converted to Christianity, the authorities in Damascus and the Turkish Wali (central government) were so incensed
that they brought great pressure on the Foreign Office to recall
Burton.[24] Accordingly, he was removed from his post—but not
until after he had managed, even during all the turmoil, to explore
many ancient ruins, in the company of a young archeologist, Charles
Tyrwhitt-Drake, which resulted in another study, *Unexplored Syria,*
coauthored and published in 1871.

Back in England, and out of a job, Burton devoted himself to
writing. A manuscript dealing with his stay in Zanzibar many years
earlier, which he thought to be irretrievably lost, was discovered
and returned to him. He reworked it and published it as a book,
Zanzibar, in 1872. Also, during the summer of that year he accepted
an offer from a British mining speculator to explore the sulpher
resources of Iceland. Nothing mineral came of that venture but
another of his two-volume studies, *Ultima Thule* (1875), one of his

least interesting works to the average reader, an encyclopedia of facts and statistics pertaining to Iceland.

Burton also produced during this period the *Two Trips to Gorilla Land and the Cataracts of the Congo* (1876), and two translations: *Lands of the Cazembe,* a book by the Portuguese explorer Lacerda (1873), and *The Captivity of Hans Stade of Hesse* (1874), translated by Albert Tootal, for which Burton wrote the introduction.

Burton had become interested in archaeology while in Damascus, and he now proceeded to pursue his new interest among the ancient Etruscan ruins in Italy. He made friends with Italian scientists and made a few minor discoveries of his own, but by and large his guidebook to the ruins, *Etruscan Bologna* (1876), was not well received—though eminent archaeologists like A. H. Sayce, Arthur Evans, and Heinrich Schliemann, the discoverer of Troy, sought him out later when he was living in Trieste.

Last Years and Last Writings

Burton spent his last years in the consulship at Trieste. It was not until this late period of his life that he revealed a side of himself that he had previously carefully concealed—the poet. He finished his translations of the *Lusiads* in 1880, the same year that saw his own best poem, *The Kasidah of Haji Abdu El-Yezdi.* Also during the 1870s he made some of his last excursions, seeking gold in the Midian desert and along the so-called "Gold Coast" of West Africa. Neither of these trips produced much gold, though once again he wrote up his experiences in two books of mediocre quality.

During the 1880s Burton's health was declining seriously. He was ill during January and February of 1884 and, in March, he suffered his first heart-attack. His condition was ominous but it did not prevent him from enjoying another six years of astonishing productivity. From 1876 until his death in 1890 he was busy finishing up projects begun earlier and working on his manuscripts and new translations of Eastern erotica, most of which he was obliged to publish privately. The last half of the nineteenth century was, of course, extremely repressive in matters of "public morality," and numerous writers and publishers were prosecuted and punished for producing works that seem amusingly harmless today—such as the English translation of Dumas's *La Dame aux Camélias* on which the popular opera *La Traviata* was based (which, incidentally, was being sung in London's Covent Garden in 1847—but its libretto was "unattainable"). In that same repressive spirit George Eliot was reprimanded in the *Saturday Review* for discussing pregnancy in her novel *Adam Bede,* and Lord Tennyson was accused by a critic of practicing adultery and fornication because these topics were mentioned in the poem *Maud* (1855). So certain critics and editors, with the support of the Obscene Publications Act of 1857 and the tireless Society for the Suppression of Vice, forced writers like Burton, who were determined not to be silenced, to go underground—in Burton's case to publish works secretly and under pseudonyms or inverted initials (B.F.R.).

During these years Burton joined forces with Foster Fitzgerald Arbuthnot, a young civil servant in India who was also a wealthy collector and talented linguist. They coauthored translations, from the Sanskrit, of Indian "manuals of love"—the *Ananga Ranga* and the *Kama Sutra*—and the Arabian treatise on sexuality, *The Perfumed Garden.* In order to get these into print Burton and Arbuthnot, with the help of Monckton Milnes, devised an ingenious publishing deception. They set up an imaginary publishing house, the Kama Shastra Society of London and Benares, with the printers said to be (conveniently out of range) in Benares, the holy city of Hinduism in northern India, or in Cosmopoli, the ancient name of the capital of the island of Elba. By using this mythic organization, and also by carefully avoiding the inflammatory use of explicit sexual language, they succeeded in being published without scandal or legal troubles.

During the late 1800s, despite suffering from many ailments and a second heart-attack, Burton continued his translations. In a remarkable outburst of creative energy he turned out ten volumes of the unexpurgated and the annotated *Arabian Nights* which, surprisingly enough, sold very well. Elated by their success, he pushed on at a furious rate, finishing six volumes of the *Supplemental Nights* in 1888. He then decided to translate an unexpurgated version of Boccaccio's *Decameron,* but on learning that a fellow translator, John Payne, had preceded him, he turned instead to a collection of earthy Neapolitan folktales, *Il Pentamerone; or the Tale of Tales,* by Giovanni Batiste Basile (1637), in which he showed that he had forgotten none of the gutter argot he had learned in Naples during his youth.

The end was to come for Burton on Sunday, 18 October 1890; but despite the increasing frailty that preceded his death, he had continued to publish—to his wife's extreme dismay and apprehension—more volumes of erotica, as if in defiance of his physical decline. He had collaborated with a young and notorious "erotic specialist," Leonard Smithers, in printing privately the first English translation of the Latin *Priapeia,* a collection of explicit poems in honor of the Greek fertility god; and Catullus' *Carmina,* a series of passionate love lyrics to the poet's mistress. He was working on a number of other erotic translations at the time of his death, and was even writing something on homosexuality and castration—again evoking the hostility of his wife Isabel.

And so the burning took place, "sorrowfully, reverently," as she put it, immediately after Burton's death, which provoked outcries of anger from many quarters. As Burton was himself vilified in the press for his "outrageous" publications, so Isabel was attacked for her display of "the bigotry of Torquemada" in her destruction of masses of her husband's manuscripts, diaries, and notes.[25] Burton had kept two sets of journals. One contained notes on his travel experiences, which included anthropological observations, summaries of books, and accounts of conversations he had had with various influential people in England. The other set consisted of his intimate diaries, which he always kept under lock and key. With the exception of a few passages Isabel kept out for quotation in her subsequent biography, the diaries were all lost. But what created the greatest outrage, especially among fellow writers who knew of Burton's work in progress, was the destruction of the manuscript of *The Scented Garden,* a reworking of the earlier Arabic manual on the "art of love," *The Perfumed Garden of Cheikh Nefzaoui,* using the original Arabic version rather than French translations, and including new materials. Burton had labored long on his new version and considered it one of his finest achievements. But Isabel, proclaiming, inaccurately, that it was a treatise on homosexual love, insisted that she was protecting her husband by burning it. She wrote several letters to the press trying to justify her actions, giving reasons that ranged from his spirit visiting her after death ordering her to burn the manuscripts, to her concern for his earthly reputation, to her determination to save his immortal soul.

Isabel also incurred great hostility for her insisting on giving Richard a Catholic funeral, thus imposing on him, after death, a faith he had rejected during life. She was doubtless moved by a genuine concern for her husband's immortal soul as well as his earthly reputation, but Richard had apparently failed utterly to foresee his wife's actions or he would never have willed Isabel his manuscripts. As one biographer says, "he had no special insight into the capacity for an unconscious revenge of a woman with a blighted sexual life. . . . She had, in truth, gone over to the enemy."[26]

Chapter Two
The Discovery of the East: India

When in 1850, after seven years in India, Burton returned to England, he was in a particularly sour frame of mind. He had spent his last months there suffering from eye infections, his assigned report on homosexual brothels in Karachi had been used against him, he had managed to incur the hostility of many of his colleagues and superiors, and he felt that he had been unjustly passed over for advancement and desirable assignments: "My career in India had been in my eyes a failure, and by no fault of my own; the dwarfish Demon called 'Interest' had fought against me, and as usual had won the fight."[1]

Burton had brought back with him, in addition to his burden of grievances, an impressive collection of materials relating to Indian life. He was fortunate in having made two good friends in India who had encouraged his first ventures into scholarship: Walter Scott, the Bombay Army engineer with whom he traveled in Sind, and Dr. John Steinhaeuser, a surgeon, a fine linguist, and an enthusiastic collector of Oriental literature. The latter first encouraged Burton to consider translating an unexpurgated version of *The Arabian Nights,* and even collaborated with him in some early drafts.

These two friends encouraged Burton to add to his own collection of Oriental books and manuscripts; he began to keep extensive journals and notes and to think seriously about writing books about India. His confidence in having something special and important to say was also strengthened when he began, in native disguise, his intelligence missions for Sir Charles Napier. He uncovered aspects of Indian life and belief that astonished his chief, which suggested to him that his discoveries might also be of interest to the English reading public. Sir Charles learned, for example, that many of the criminals he hanged were poverty-stricken substitutes hired for the occasion by the convicted rich. And certain grim facts were revealed about wife killing by jealous husbands, along with the practice of killing unwanted daughters, as among the Todas of the Goa mountains, whose infant daughters were sometimes drowned in milk or trampled to death by water buffaloes. Among the Belochis the girls were often killed by opium. Burton pointed out that this infanticide was usually carried out in cases of "illegitimate" daughters.[2] Reports like these, dealing with the more colorful and sensational aspects of Oriental society, were sure to find an audience back in England.

Burton Becomes a Writer

Burton's first efforts at becoming a published writer were anything but sensational; they took the form of two technical papers based on his linguistic studies in Sind, and two papers on the Sindians themselves that were brief exploratory attempts at the new science of ethnology. The papers were published, in 1849 and 1855, in local journals in Bombay and were later absorbed into his full-length books on Sind.[3]

Earlier, in 1847, Burton had revealed his urge toward creative scholarship when he began translating the popular fables of Pilpay, the "Indian Aesop." This, his first translation, was never published, but he produced a 100-page manuscript before discontinuing the project.[4]

The Books on India

Back in England Burton divided his time between flirting with the local ladies and writing his four books on India,[5] all published in 1851–52, in less than two years—which has no doubt accounted for some of the negative criticism the books received. These works varied in size and content but had one thing in common: they were unsuccessful—they did not sell well nor elicit much favorable comment from contemporary critics. More recently, opinion as to their qualities has been sharply divided. These four books also had another quality in common: they conveyed a tone of disenchantment, especially the first three. Due in part to his "unfair" treatment while in India and in part to his disillusionment on first viewing the fabulous Orient, Burton's first books are characterized by contrasts between expectations and reality. On his arrival in India Burton was struck primarily by the dinginess, filth, and foul odors; he noted with disgust the open sewers, the stench of the Hindu funeral burning-grounds, and the lizards, rats, and congestion—all of which, however, did not prevent him from flinging himself eagerly into local native life. But this disenchantment, at least in aesthetic terms, is apparent, for example, in the opening pages of *Goa,* when he is describing the Indian town of Bombahia:

> Thirdly, convert bright Naples, with its rows of white palazzi, its romantic-looking forts, its beautiful promenade, and charming background into a low, black, dirty port, *et voici* the magnificent Bombahia. You may, it is true, attempt to get up a little romance about the "fairy caves" of Salsette and Elephanta, the tepid seas, the spicy breeze, and the ancient and classical name of Momba-devi.
> But you'll fail. (6)

And here he concluded his impressions of the town of Seroda:

> Reader, we have been minute, perhaps unnecessarily so, in describing our visit to Seroda. If you be one of those who take no interest in a traveller's "feeds," his sufferings from vermin, or his "rows about the bill," you will have found the preceding pages uninteresting enough. Our object is, however, to give you a plain programme of what entertainment you may expect from the famed town of the Bayaderes, and, should your footsteps be ever likely to wander in that direction, to prepare you for the disappointment you will infallibly incur. (134–35)

On the other hand, Burton seems at times to enjoy his disenchantment. He describes with great zest the hazards of primitive forms of travel, the physical and human obstacles to be challenged and overcome, and he narrates his adventures with humor and irony.[6] This is especially true of the first two books, on Goa and Sind, where he addresses the reader in familiar and even colloquial terms.

Goa and the Blue Mountains;
or, Six Months of Sick Leave

Goa (1851) is primarily an account of a visit to the former Portuguese colony of that name, and it introduces the reader to varied inhabitants: the converted "black Christians," the Hindus of Malabar, the Moslems of Panjim, the wretched "Mestici, or mixed breed who compose the great mass of society of Goa," and the mountain-dwelling Todas who practiced polyandry. *Goa* also introduces the reader to what will be the prevailing style and structure of Burton's works—a curious and rather experimental approach to his material that will make reading the books a more arduous experience than Burton probably intended; for, as will be discussed later, Burton seemed unsure of what kind of books he wanted to write and what kind of audience they were intended for.

The substance of *Goa* is a typical Burton melange: pages of personal narrative and anecdote, descriptions of modes of travel (all uncomfortable), conditions of life at British hill-stations, the history of Goa under its Portuguese rulers, with emphasis on the horrors of the Inquisition; discussions of the various races, their appearance, beliefs, customs, and daily life; commentary in technical terms on the topography, local fauna, agriculture, meteorological conditions, rudimentary industries, and, always, learned discussions of local languages and dialects. The book can be very engaging at times, and can become formidably heavy-going at others. The reader can skip, if he so chooses, the more technical and specialized passages, but it is hard to overlook one of Burton's most prominent characteristics: the unrestrained display of personal opinion and prejudice, a harshness of value judgment, the tendency to denigrate both the darker races and Europeans he does not happen to like, and a seeming lack of compassion for the wretched of the earth. After describing the strong antipathies between the various Goan races, for instance, he stresses his personal hostility to mixed marriages, mixed religions, religious converts, and mixed races—the "mongrel men" about whom Burton says: "It would be, we believe, difficult to find in Asia an uglier or more degraded race than that which we are now describing." With his usual generous detail Burton then describes the ugly mongrel (97–98). This practice—of depicting in sharp detail a general type, or stereotype—will be a pervasive feature of Burton's "ethnography," and we will have occasion to question his penchant for generalizing and reducing human beings to categories and classes.[7]

Of the business of converting the Indians to Christianity, whether by force or gentler persuasion, Burton has much to say, as he will later in his books on Africa. He takes a dim, and usually sardonic, view of the practice: "These Hindoos very rarely become Christians, now that fire and steel, the dungeon and the rack, the rice-pot and the rupee, are not allowed to play the persuasive part in the good work formerly assigned to them." And when a conversion does take place, it is accompanied by "all the pomp and ceremony due to the importance of spoiling a good Gentoo by making a bad Christian of him" (109). Later he observes that "What Goa has done may serve as a lesson to us. She compelled or induced good Hindoos and Moslems to become bad Christians. The consequence has been the utter degeneracy of the breed, who have been justly characterized by our House of Commons as 'a race the least respected and respectable, and the least fitted for soldiers of all the tribes that diversify the populous country of India' " (156).

Regarding mixing the races, Burton held theories which seem dubious to readers in the 1980s, but which were accepted "science" of his day. He asserts, for example, that the offspring will "degenerate after the second generation." This is especially true of the "Hindoos" who are "the lowest branch of the Caucasian or Iranian family." Because of the "mental inferiority of the mixed breed . . . neither British nor Portuguese India ever produced a half-caste at all deserving of being ranked in the typical order of man" (156–57). And in his chapter on the "Moslems of Malabar" Burton will have similar caustic things to say, these Moslems' inferiority also deriving from their being a "mixed breed," sprung from the promiscuous relations that took place between the first Arab settlers and the women of the country (230–31). This is typical Burton, passing out his prejudices as if they were scientific fact.

There are, fortunately, other sides of Burton more to his credit. When personal opinion is restrained, he can treat the reader to a lively and fascinating close-up of the daily lives, beliefs, and customs of the Indian peoples of the regions he visited. He did, after all, have access to places and experiences denied to most Europeans, and he took copious and usually accurate notes (according to other and subsequent observers). But very often his descriptions combine relatively objective reporting with personal value judgments:

The only peculiarity in the Moplah lady's costume is the horrible ornamenting of the ear. At an early age the lobe is pierced, and a bit of lead, or a piece of Shola wood is inserted in order to enlarge the orifice. After a time the lobe becomes about the size of a crown piece, and a circle of gold, silver, or palm-leaf, dyed red, white, or yellow, is inserted into it—the distended skin of the lobe containing and surrounding the ring. There is something peculiarly revolting to a stranger's eye in the appearance of the two long strips of flesh instead of ears, which hang down on each side of the head in old age, when ornaments are no longer worn. (232–33)

This passage is representative of the close observation which forms the basis of Burton's descriptions; it also shows his tendency to use emotionally loaded language. That is, terms such as "peculiarity," "horrible," and "revolting" are typical examples of Burton's cultural bias as well as of his wish to give the sincere reactions which he believed would be experienced by any ordinary English person on witnessing the described scene for himself. Also typical is his tendency to choose for description the more sensational aspects of the peoples of the region. Speaking of the Moplah, one of the Moslem groups of Malabar, Burton tells us:

> Sometimes half a dozen desperadoes will arm themselves, seize upon a substantial house, and send a message of defiance to the collector of the district. Their favourite weapon on such occasions is the long knife that usually hangs from the waist: when entering battle they generally carry two, one in the hand, and the other between the teeth. They invariably prepare themselves for combat by a powerful dose of hemp or opium, fight to the last with frenzied obstinacy, despise the most dreadful wounds, and continue to exert themselves when a European would be quite disabled— a peculiarity which they probably inherit from their Arab ancestors. Like the Malay when he runs a-muck, these men never think of asking for, or giving quarter; they make up their minds to become martyrs, and only try to attain high rank in that glorious body by slaying as many infidels as they can. (238)

Burton, like Kipling after him, was always willing to admire a "lesser breed" when he showed valor and ability in military or personal combat. When describing his own experiences in India, Burton often resorts to a rather heavy humor which is obviously intended to entertain. The following is typical—an account of overland travel in a *palanquin,* a kind of box attached to poles carried on the shoulders of native bearers:

> We cannot promise you much pleasure in the enjoyment of this celebrated Oriental luxury. Between your head and the glowing sun, there is scarcely half an inch of plank, covered with a thin mat, which ought to be, but never is, watered. After a day or two you will hesitate which to hate the most, your bearers' monotonous, melancholy, grunting, groaning chaunt, when fresh, or their jolting, jerking, shambling, staggering gait, when tired. In a perpetual state of low fever you cannot eat, drink, or sleep; your mouth burns, your head throbs, your back aches, and your temper borders upon the ferocious. (251)

Burton often uses the techniques of fiction to enhance his narrative; at times he resorts completely to storytelling. His books include many such (tall?) tales. One of Burton's better stories (whether it qualifies as "fiction" or not is open to question) regards an adventurous attempt to kidnap a lovely young nun who was serving as a Latin professor in an Indian nunnery. Her eyes and demeanor had suggested—at least to Burton—that an abduction would not be entirely repugnant to her. Burton does not, however, tell the story in his own voice. He had it recounted to him by a native servant named "Salvator" (the choice of name will be significant), who purported to be describing the exploits of his own "Sahib." Biographers are reasonably sure that the "Sahib" was Burton himself; it is another example, of which there will be many, of Burton's tendency to disguise himself in one way or another, to use an assumed name or identity.

The story provides a good example of the author in one of his lighter artistic moods, and "Salvator" narrates the preparations for the planned abduction by his master and his chosen companion "that ruffian Khudadah." He tells how the abduction party met at midnight and, after scaling walls and groping around in the dark unfamiliar corridors of the nunnery, succeed in gathering up the young woman and bearing her off "in triumph." Once safely outside the walls, they examine their prize: "Imagine his horror and disgust when, instead of the expected large black eyes and the pretty little rose-bud of a mouth, a pair of rolling yellow balls glared fearfully in his face, and two big black lips, at first shut with terror, began to shout and scream with all their might. 'Khudadah, we have eaten filth,' said my master, 'how are we to lay this she-devil?' " They decided, after a moment's consideration, that cutting her throat "won't do." So they gag and pinion their inadvertant victim, leave her where she lay, board their ship, and sail off (82–85).

In the next paragraph, Burton resumes his scholarly persona: "The population of Goa is composed of three heterogeneous elements, namely, pure Portuguese, black Christians, and the heathenry. A short description of each order will, perhaps, be acceptable to the reader."

Scinde; or, The Unhappy Valley

The second book, *Scinde; or, The Unhappy Valley* (1851),[8] was similarly written to entertain as well as to inform. The style, for the most part, is again informal, sardonic, at times even chatty. The book is dedicated to Lieutenant-Colonel Walter Scott but the narrator addresses himself to "Mr. John Bull" who is invited to accompany him through the province of Sind in northwest India. Burton frequently interrupts his narrative to lecture Mr. Bull directly, to point out something to him, confide in him, or perhaps reprimand him for his presumed inability to fully comprehend or appreciate some fine point.

The narrative begins with a short sea voyage up the western coast of India to Sind in a picturesque native ship. This craft, called a "Patimar," and its colorful captain, crew, and many of the travelers, seem more appropriate to the days of Sinbad than to the mid-nineteenth century. It is from this, "The 'Shippe of Helle'—i.e., The Government Steamer," that the passengers gain their first view of the "unhappy valley" and the town of "Kurrachee." From there the travelers move inland and Burton proceeds with his usual combination of history, ethnology, linguistics, and personal anecdote. Some of the most interesting chapters are those that include Burton's recounting of Indian legends and folktales—"Shaykh Radhan and the Dead Camel" and "The Seven Headless Prophets"—often juxtaposed with contemporary events involving the British or the author himself, such as amorous episodes with native women or learning to ride wild alligators bareback (both equally hazardous enterprises).

In this work Burton will start coming into his own as an anthropologist. The personal judgments are still there, but so are many careful descriptions of the Sindians, presented close-up, as in the chapter devoted to "A Belochi Dinner and Tea-Party," "Shikarpur, its Central Asian Bazaar, and its Hindoos," "The Hindoos of Scinde—Their Rascality and their Philoprogenitiveness," "The Scindian Man—His Character and What He Drinks," "The Scindian Woman—Especially Her Exterior." Burton makes many harsh judgments but he also finds much to praise; and he begins a practice that he will follow in all his travel books—that of comparing the "barbarian" customs with those of "civilized" Europe, and not always to the advantage of the Europeans. For example, after observing that many of the Hindu women in Sind are very pretty, fond of pleasure, and given to flirting, he concludes that they are also admirable wives and mothers:

They are good, hard-working, and affectionate wives. Their love for their offspring, the great female virtue in the East, is an all-absorbing passion, beautiful, despite of its excess. To the Hindoo mother her child is everything. From the hour of his birth she never leaves him day or night. If poor, she works, walking about with him on her hip; if rich, she spends life with him on her lap. When he is in health she passes her time in kneading, and straightening his limbs. When he is sick, she fasts and watches, and endures every self-imposed penance she can devise. She never speaks to or of him without imploring the blessing of Heaven upon his head; and this strong love loses naught when the child ceases to be a toy; it is the mainspring of her conduct towards him throughout life. No wonder that in the East an unaffectionate son is a rare phenomenon: and no wonder that this people when offensively inclined always begin by abusing one another's mothers.

Having made his point, Burton then turns his disapproving attention to his presumed British reader: "Own to me, Mr. Bull, if you have candour enough, that in this point at least civilisation gains nothing by contrast with barbarism. The parents are engrossed by other cares—the search for riches, or the pursuit of pleasure— during the infancy of their offspring. In the troublesome days of childhood the boy is consigned to a nursery, or let loose to pass his time with his fellows as he best can; then comes youth accompanied by an exile to school and college; then the profession; then the marriage; and the 'young family'—a *coup de grâce*."[9]

In this passage, what begins as a description ends as an editorial. This is an aspect of Burton's desire to educate his readers. The point can be made that while Burton seems to be racially biased and judgmental, he is usually "democratic" in his criticism. He was by temperament a critic and fault-finder, and, as we have seen, he can be very abrasive—and not just toward the natives of the countries he explored. He was intolerant of anybody, anywhere, who seemed to him ignorant or incompetent. He tried to keep his books non-political, but he occasionally jeered, with heavy irony, at an institution he was really quite devoted to—British imperialism: "Whenever good Madam Britannia is about to break the eighth commandment, she simultaneously displays a lot of piety, much rhapsodising about the bright dawn of Christianity, the finger of Providence, the spread of civilisation, and the infinite benefits conferred upon the barbarians by permitting them to become her subjects, and pay their rents to her" (1:182). What Burton is railing at here, however, is not the idea of imperialism itself, but aspects of its implementation—hypocrisy, solemn piety, and the confusion of spiritual and commercial objectives.

Sindh and the Races that Inhabit the Valley of the Indus

Sindh and the Races that Inhabit the Valley of the Indus; with Notices of the Topography and History of the Province (1851)[10] is, as its full title indicates, an ambitious book. Its table of contents is awesome in scope and diversity of topics, which include, in addition to Sind's topography and history, its value as a military and commercial region, its system of canals and taxation, lists of Sindi legends and languages, biographies of celebrated Sindi authors, and detailed accounts of Sindi customs and domestic life. Speaking of the domestic life, Burton assures the reader that he "has striven to the utmost to avoid all unnecessary indelicacy; but in minute descriptions of the manners and customs of a barbarous or semi-civilized race, it is, as every traveler knows, impossible to preserve a work completely pure" (xxii).

Unfortunately, many of his English reviewers found his books to be highly impure. In this and other early works, Burton chafed under the restrictions placed on him by timorous publishers and other determiners of the English reading-public's tastes. Nevertheless, he did his best, he said, to depict, hopefully without offending, such matters as birth, circumcision rites, betrothal and nuptial ceremonies, death and burial customs, along with even more dangerous topics—"The Customs of Females: their Morals, Habits, Intrigues and Dress—The Dancing Girls, Prostitutes, and Musicians." Burton has been especially praised, in recent times, for his portrayal of Sindi marriage customs and for his learned chapter on the religion and literature of the Sufis.[11] The book may also have attracted readers interested in such subjects as "The Occult Sciences, Demonology, Magic and Alchemy—Osteomancy, the Book of Fate—Oneiromancy—Palmistry—Omens—Crimes and their Punishments."

Falconry in the Valley of the Indus

Burton's fourth book on India is relatively quick and easy reading. *Falconry in the Valley of the Indus* (1852) is a short work on the "art," or "sport," of hunting wild game with trained falcons, and it contains some commentaries on native life and customs. The author, in a brief introductory history of falconry, reveals his love for the sport along with an impressive knowledge of its fine points: the various kinds of falcons and hawks and the techniques of raising and training the creatures, and he takes the reader on some hunting excursions in company with an Indian nobleman devoted to the pastime. It may not be to everyone's taste, but Burton gives an exciting account of a day's hunting with the birds. The principal source of interest in the book, however—at least for Burton's biographers—is the lengthy postscript that provides revealing material on Burton's living in and writing about India, but which also reveals interesting information on Burton's narrative technique.

The postscript begins with a response to Burton's critics, especially to one who, after patting Burton on the head for at least trying to study and understand the Indians, takes him to task for "some very extreme opinions" and for lacking "moderation" which the critic finds unseemly "for such a young man." (Burton was "merely" a lieutenant and barely thirty years old.) Burton, betraying his usual sensitivity to adverse criticism, cites a number of critical comments favorable to his work, and then launches into an autobiographical narrative designed to establish his credentials. He admits to his unsuccessful university days, then talks about his experiences learning the languages and cultures of the East Indians, especially those in Sind. He relates how, after he had mastered Persian, Arabic, and Hindustani, and had "a superficial knowledge of that dialect of Punjaubee which is spoken in the wilder part of the province, I began the systematic study of the Scindian people, their manners and their tongue. The first difficulty was to pass for an Oriental, and this was as necessary as it was difficult" (98–99).

Here Burton reveals one of the several reasons he studied the East Indians so closely and wrote about them so minutely. He was convinced that one the main obstacles to British success in India was ignorance, and at the cost of showing his contempt for most of his fellow officers and superiors, he proceeded, in all sincerity, to bridge the dangerous gap of ignorance.

The European official in Indian seldom, if ever, sees anything in its real light, so dense is the veil which the fearfulness, the duplicity, the prejudice and the superstitions of the natives hang before his eyes. And the white man lives a life so distinct from the black, that hundreds of the former serve through what they call their "term of exile," without once being present at a circumcision feast, a wedding, or a funeral. More especially the present generation, whom the habit and the means of taking furloughs, the increased facility for enjoying ladies' society, and, if truth be spoken, a greater regard for appearances if not a stricter code of morality, estrange from their dusky fellow subjects every day and day the more. (99)[12]

He describes why his best disguise would be that of a traveling merchant, half-Arab and half-Iranian (Persian), which would account for any slight accent or variation in manner. Since India was populated with every conceivable kind of racial mixture and hundreds of languages and dialects, the danger of his being detected, Burton asserts, "was a very inconsiderable one." With great relish he describes his masquerade, drawing, as was his habit, on the devices of fiction, and telling the story in the third person. This seems appropriate since the protagonist, in a real sense, is someone other than Captain Richard Burton:

With hair falling upon his shoulders, a long beard, face and hands, arms and feet, stained with a thin coat of henna, Mirza Abdullah of Bushire—your humble servant, gentle reader—set out upon many and many a trip. He was a Bazzaz, a vender of fine linen, calicoes and muslins;—such chapmen are sometimes admitted to display their wares even in the sacred harem by "fast" and fashionable dames.

Thus he could walk into most men's houses quite without ceremony;— even if the master dreamed of kicking him out, the mistress was sure to oppose such measure with might and main. He secured numberless invitations, was proposed to by several papas, and won, or had to think he won, a few hearts; for he came as a rich man and he stayed with dignity, and he departed exacting all the honours. When wending his ways he usually urged a return of visit in the morning, but he was seldom to be found at the caravanserai he specified—was Mirza Abdullah the Bushiri. (100)

Burton continues with the adventures of "Mirza" for several pages, concluding with "What scenes he saw! What adventures he went through! But who would believe, even if he ventured to detail them?"

Fortunately Burton details a few of them, and he tells of his pleasant hours in the home of an elderly Moslem matron who had befriended him. The occasions of his resting in her garden are full of the exotic smells and sounds of the East. Here, in the last pages of his fourth book, all traces of disenchantment with the Orient have vanished. He has discovered the culture into which he settles most comfortably—the Moslem world that he will explore more deeply in the years to come: "So it often happened that Mirza Abdullah was turned out of the house to pass a few hours in the garden. There he sat upon his felt rug spread beneath a shadowy tamarind, with beds of sweet-smelling basil around him, his eyes roving over the broad river that coursed rapidly between its wooded banks and the groups gathered at the frequent ferries, whilst the soft strains of mysterious, philosophical, transcendental Hafiz were sounded in his ears by the other Meerza, his companion, Mohammed Hosayn—peace be upon him!" (105).

Burton concludes his postscript by returning to his more difficult role—that of Captain Burton—and to his defense against his critics.

Burton's Intentions and Critics' Reactions

Burton's main intention in writing these books was to bring the East, accurately and authentically, to the West, for the latter's edification. He is probably at his best when showing the impact of one culture upon another, Moslem upon Hindu, Portuguese upon Indian, Indian upon British. Some of his most interesting stories deal with the sort of intercultural misunderstandings that he hoped to rectify. A good example is his tale of the British colonel and the drowning Sindian. The colonel sees a native floundering in a river and orders local workmen to save him. When none springs to the rescue, he strikes at them with a whip instead of, more efficaciously, offering them a rupee—to which, Burton assures us, they would have responded instantly. The Sindians scatter and the colonel is forced to dive into the water himself. Once rescued, the Sindian offers no thanks, but says, "Sahib, you have preserved me, what are you going to give me?" The Englishman, recoiling in anger, refused him charity, whereupon the native begins cursing him. The story ends with the now thoroughly outraged officer swinging his whip at the man whose life he has just saved (54).

This story does make its point: there is indeed a breakdown of mutual understanding, in which none of the parties to the event is shown to any particular advantage. But Burton is content to let the example stand; he does not illuminate the cultural issues at work here—the view, not exclusive to the Indian race, that in saving one's life one incurs a responsibility to him. Here Burton leaves the reader in the same darkness in which the colonel finds himself; in other instances, as we have seen, Burton will provide the edifying commentary.

Burton's books on India are full of interesting information about exotic parts of the world; they include something for everyone, whether one's interests are history, anthropology, language, or just touristing through fascinating strange lands; and they are written in a vigorous style that can entertain even when the reader does not agree with what is being said. Then why, one may legitimately ask, were the books failures? One must surely consider a failure a book like *Falconry:* 500 copies were printed and twenty-five years later his publishers reported to him that 257 copies were still unsold. [13] The books on Sind and Goa did not fare much better. The reviews of the books were not all unkind, but the reviewers seemed unsure of what to say about works that contained, to their Victorian minds, material that was often repellent and offensive to good taste. Many reviewers were, in Burton's opinion, unperceptive, ignorant, and patronizing, and he did not hesitate to say so. The comments already cited from the postscript of *Falconry* were directed at the usually genial editor of the influential journal *Athenaeum,* who retaliated by commenting, in an almost libelous fashion, on Burton's habit of living with the natives.

One can understand that prudish editors and critics of that era were frightened by what Burton wanted them to praise, for they were not accustomed to books that discussed not only matters like irrigation, taxation, classification of tribes and castes, and education and religious beliefs, but also the primordial rituals—birth and lactation superstitions and practices, circumcision and puberty ceremonies, marriage rites, punishments (usually drastic) for adultery, aphrodisiacs, sexual responsiveness in women, and complicated rituals for the dead. Burton, in dealing with these "indelicate" aspects of Indian life, thought he was being restrained and prudent, and indeed he was, when compared with what he would write in later years, but it was still too rich a mixture for many of his critics and readers.

Moreover, even readers who might be attracted to his books could find failings of other types, especially those of style and form. The passages quoted in the preceding pages probably show the author at his best. When Burton set out to tell a story, to entertain, his

writing was usually lively and lucid; but when he decided to become
the scholar, his style often became murky, verging on the impen-
etrable, largely because of his apparent need to impress the reader
with his erudition and his awesome vocabulary. He loved to coin
new words, and some of them seem clear and useful enough: "con-
versationalizing," "re-became," and "us-wards." But his fondness
for esoteric, foreign, and archaic words can become annoying: "na-
tation" for swimming, "piscation" for fishing, "quadruped creation"
for horse, and one expression that deserves a special award—"five
venerable proceeds of the cow" which translates as cow dung. The
many obscure allusions he strews along the way can become stum-
bling-blocks, as he rarely explains them, and at times he is simply
verbose. He delights in multisyllabic words, and in the first few
chapters of *Scinde, or the Unhappy Valley* the reader confronts such
terms as "triduan," "catalepsed," "futilised," "graveolent," "ses-
quipedalian," "agnomen," "confabulate," "succedaneum," "vaticin-
ating," "cachinnatory," and "vellication." Even *Goa,* supposedly
written for popular consumption, contains words, phrases, and quo-
tations in Portuguese, Hindustani, Arabic, French, Latin, Persian,
Greek, Italian, and Sanskrit.

Burton also loved footnotes—hundreds of them—and he seemed
to be quite comfortable with them. In fact, some of his best writing
appears in the small print at the bottom of the page, and sometimes
the footnotes exceed in length the main text on the page. The reason
for this pedantry seems apparent. Burton was understandably concerned that his integrity as a scholar be respected. He had, after
all, failed to get his university degree; furthermore, he was known
in his social life as a teller of tall tales, and in his writings he was
proud of his talent for disguise and assumed identities. Thus he had
to prove that while guilty of some personal dissimulation, he was
meticulously exact in his description of native peoples. He ended
Falconry by pointing out how easy it was in the East to create
"extreme confusion of Fact and Fiction" (87), and he provided proof,
inordinant quantities of proof, in support of his assertions. In *Sindh
and the Races that Inhabit the Valley of the Indus* there are five appendixes, a large detailed map, and 599 footnotes.

The sheer quantity of materials that Burton poured into his books
on India was an obstacle to some readers, while evoking admiration
in others. Isabel Burton, characteristically, was delighted with her
husband's first book on Scinde: *"Scinde, or the Unhappy Valley* is, I

think, the freshest, most witty and spirited thing I ever read. He had not been at war with the critics and Mrs. Grundy then, and there is all the boy's fun and fire in it."[14] One of Burton's major biographers, however, sees it differently. He refers to "all the literary and philosophical rubbish in these early books," and complains that "as with most of his travel books, the contents of his bulging notebooks were simply dumped into his manuscripts with no apparent editing . . . with little regard to order or appropriateness."[15] Another scholar, on the other hand, says of *Sindh:* "Indeed one may choose at random any chapter in the book, and having read it run through all that had been previously written on that subject; in every instance Burton's minute knowledge will be found to throw into the shade the sum of all that had been recorded by his predecessors."[16]

This divergence of critical opinion exemplifies a common source of division among Burton's commentators: the first critic is not questioning the factual authenticity of Burton's India books; he is emphasizing, on aesthetic grounds, the *manner* in which the content is conveyed to the reader. The second critic is emphasizing the content itself. One of Burton's failings as a writer is that he lacked a clear sense of audience. He wanted to reach a wide reading public, yet he used a language and technique often designed to thwart readers who did not share his expertise or his zest for the esoteric and arcane. It is also possible that his lack of popular literary success was due to his expressing, on many occasions, an undisguised contempt for his readers. In those passages directly addressed to "Mr. John Bull," for instance, the reader is often made to appear naive, uninformed, even stupid—if, that is, the reader identifies with Mr. Bull. If he can perceive Mr. Bull as referring to most *other* readers, and can skip, skim, prove adaptable to shifts in tone and style, pick and choose as individual interest leads, he can find Burton's books on India to be illuminating and entertaining; but in no way do they attain the quality of the next books he was to write—those on Arabia and Africa.

Chapter Three
The Discovery
of the East: Arabia

Although Burton began his study of the Arabic language while he was still in England, it was during his seven-year sojourn in India that he discovered his love for the Islamic culture. He studied and described the other religions and cultures of that vast land, but it was only when garbed as an Arab, sitting in fragrant gardens under tamarind and olive trees, sipping coffee, and discussing the finer points of the *Koran,* that a certain peace seemed to descend upon him. It is reflected in his style of writing: at these times the judgmental edge is often dulled, the craggy roughness of phrasing is smoothed, the tone mellows, and a sense of romance glows through every word. For it is in his experiences among the Moslems that Burton's innate romanticism surfaces—and so it was probably inevitable that he would resolve to make the pilgrimage, to have the supreme adventure of becoming a *Haji,* one who has traveled to the sacred cities and worshipped at the holy shrines in Mecca and Medina.

Of all the many languages Burton mastered, his favorites were Arabic and Persian. He found in them an emotional and poetic richness that bordered on the erotic—in fact, he took to language "as other men took to liquor and women, intoxicated by the sense of mastery and the exhilaration of unlocking mysteries." It is possible that linguistic mysteries were a substitute for more primitive mysteries—that foreign tongues had for him a "libidinal" quality, particularly since he grew up without a true mother tongue. The Arabic language, which he came to cherish above all others, he described as "a faithful wife following the mind and giving birth to its offspring" (2:100).[1]

Arabia: The European Fantasy

Burton's fascination with the far shores of Araby was shared by Europeans whose imaginations had been fed since Marco Polo by fabulous Oriental tales,[2] including early versions of *The Arabian Nights* which were read, assimilated, and quoted by most literate persons.[3] The European mind was also fed by the well-publicized exploits of Empire, military adventures such as Clive in India and Napoleon's invasion of Egypt, the stories brought back by early travelers in the Middle East, and perhaps, most important of all, the celebration of the Exotic East by the artists and writers of the Romantic Era. They had created vivid and largely idealized myths and legends of Eastern cultures in general, and of the picturesque desert lands of Araby in particular. Much of the literature of the early nineteenth century sparkled with exotic Oriental jewels and was redolent of spice and langorous perfumes; poetry shimmered with desert moonlight and was intoxicated by forbidden opiates, enchanted by tinkling camel bells and harem gongs, heady with the lush sensuality imagined to pervade the free and easy lives of the sheiks and dark-eyed dancing girls who lived south and east of the Mediterranean. On the Continent many French writers— including Gerard de Nerval, Baudelaire, Gautier, and Flaubert— traveled in the East and enriched their literature with the sights, sounds, and odors of the Orient, while in England such poets as Byron, Shelley, Coleridge, and Southey celebrated the exciting blend of medieval chivalry, bold adventure, and sexual license that comprised their poetic conception of the East. Even the proper Victorians, many of whom took a dubious view of the poetry and social ideas of the romantics, nevertheless provided an enthusiastic market for the tales and travel stories emanating from the eastern lands.

Burton, who was in many ways a product of the Romantic Era, attempted to clarify the legends, to bring the "true" Arabia out of the idealized myths; but what he actually did was to confirm, in more solid detail, what Europe had already come to believe about those remote regions. At the beginning of Southey's *Thalaba the Destroyer* (1801), for example, we are given a typical view of the perfect Arabian night:

> No mist obscures, nor cloud, nor speck, nor stain,
> Breaks the serene of heaven;
> In full-orb'd glory yonder Moon divine
> Rolls through the dark-blue depths.
> Beneath her steady ray
> The desert-circle spreads,

> Like the round ocean, girdled with sky. . . .
> No station is in view,
> No palm-grove, islanded amid the waste.

Eighty-four years later, in the foreword to his translation of *The Arabian Nights* (1885), Burton also describes the splendors of the desert night. It is the same desert but to the aura of magical romance is added the factual detail: "Once more I saw the evening star hanging like a solitaire from the pure front of the western firmament; and the afterglow transfiguring and transforming, as if by magic, the homely and rugged features of the scene into a fairy-land lit with a light which never shines on other soils or seas. Then would appear the woollen tents, low and black, of the true Badawin, mere dots in the boundless waste of lion-tawny clays and gazelle-brown gravels, and the camp-fire dotting like a glow-worm the village centre" (1:vii–viii).

Personal Narrative of a Pilgrimage to Meccah and El-Medinah

Burton's *Pilgrimage to Meccah and El-Medinah* (1855–56) found a ready audience. It created quite a sensation; it was widely read and acclaimed and afforded its author the stature he had failed to find with his books on India. *Pilgrimage* provided information as well as adventure, facts as well as romance, and it provided a hero—a protagonist of dauntless courage and awesome intellectual resources who might have been created by Byron himself—in the form of its colorful narrator. For the story is only partly about Arabia and its mysteries; it is also about the person, the thoughts and ideas, the emotions and attitudes, of Richard Burton. Everything is seen and described in detail, but it is also shaped, classified, and evaluated by the omnipresent sensibility of the narrator. Many travel writers have attempted, or pretended, to be totally objective. Burton, as usual, will be scholarly, will support his assertions with all the evidence he can muster, but he will not deny his own presence in the landscape. It is *his* eyes, ears, and nose which are registering, his hands surreptitiously scribbling notes, his crabbed handwriting which will be transformed into a book, and his life which is on the line during the entire experience. He is very much in the center of the stage, controlling the action, directing the drama, and arranging his experiences for the purposes of his narrative. Burton seems constantly aware of an audience and of the image he is presenting.

So in addition to the "Ruffian Dick" image that followed him from India, there now emerged a new and larger figure—created partly by his own rather theatrical manner and enhanced, after his death, by his admiring wife Isabel, who, in her preface to the memorial edition of *Pilgrimage* (1893), contributed generously to the popular mythology that was growing up around her husband. Burton himself had been content to describe his exploits colorfully, but also as they actually happened. He never claimed, for example, to have been the first white European to have gained entrance to the Arabian holy cities. In fact, he makes a point of citing his predecessors, especially the Swiss Burkhardt, and he frequently compares his observations with those of the earlier travelers. Isabel does not claim explicitly that Burton's achievement was the first of its kind, but she is quite willing to let that strong suggestion emerge— and it soon became the popular belief. She is partly correct, however—it is true that Burton's exploit was one that few could attempt, and no doubt fewer survive.

Preparations for the pilgrimage.   Burton began his pilgimage in Alexandria. He describes how he reverted to his former Indian guise of "Mirza Abdullah, Persian merchant," and he spent several weeks perfecting his language, his appearance, his knowledge and practice of the numerous social and religious observances that would mark him, to any observant Moslem, as a true believer—or not. His capacity for observing traits of human behavior was that of an actor studying a part. He shows us, for instance, the Indian Moslem's proper way of drinking a glass of water:

With us the operation is simple enough, but his performance includes no fewer than five novelties. In the first place he clutches his tumbler as though it were the throat of a foe; secondly, he ejaculates, "In the name of Allah the Compassionate, the Merciful!" before wetting his lips; thirdly, he imbibes the contents, swallowing them, not sipping them as he ought to do, and ending with a satisfied grunt; fourthly, before setting down the cup, he sighs forth "Praise be to Allah!"—of which you will understand the full meaning in the desert; and fifthly, he replies, "May Allah make it pleasant to thee!" in answer to his friend's polite "Pleasurably and health!" (1:6)

He also decided to add to his titles that of dervish (darwaysh) and physican, as he had acquired a passable knowledge of Eastern medical practice and dervish demeanor. As he explains it:

No character in the Moslem world is so proper for disguise as that of Darwaysh. It is assumed by all ranks, ages and creeds; by the nobleman who has been disgraced at court, and by the peasant who is too idle to till the ground; by Dives, who is weary of life, and by Lazarus, who begs his way from door to door. Further, the Darwaysh is allowed to ignore ceremony and politeness, as one who ceases to appear upon the stage of life; he may pray or not, marry or remain single as he pleases, be respectable in the cloth of frieze as in cloth of gold, and no one asks him—the chartered vagabond—why he comes here? or wherefore he goes there? (1:14–15)

And Burton adds happily, with self-insight: "The more haughty and offensive he is to people, the more they respect him; a decided advantage to the traveller of choleric temperament." It is by touches like these, here suggesting his own volatile emotions, that Burton, even while maintaining sharpness and accuracy of observation, contrives to remain on the center of the stage.

His narrative abounds in dramatic episodes which he describes in full-bodied prose, and despite the high seriousness both of his purposes and his view of himself, there is always the irony and sense of humor to enhance his story. Once, when in need of a visa, he is introduced to the head of the Afghan College at the Azhar Mosque: "a little, thin, ragged-bearded, one-eyed, hare-lipped divine [who] refused pipes and coffee, professing to be ascetically disposed; but he ate more than half my dinner, to reassure me, I presume, should I have been fearful that abstinence might injure his health" (1:130). And he describes in detail the progress of a drinking bout with Ali Agha, a wild-looking captain of the Albanian Irregulars, which ends with that moustachioed warrior being dragged, yelling challenge and abuse at all Egyptians, to his bed. Burton comments, "No Welsh undergraduate at Oxford, under similar circumstances, ever gave more trouble" (1:132–39).

The pilgrimage begins. Following this and other little adventures in Egypt, Burton embarked on his journey to Arabia. His book describes his traveling overland to Suez, where he took a ship south through the Red Sea to the Arabian coastal town of Yanbo. From there he traveled inland to Medina, then swung south on the long and dangerous trek to Mecca. His plans after that were uncertain, but, as it turned out, he felt after reaching Mecca that his pilgrimage had been completed; so he returned west to the Red Sea and caught a ship back to Cairo. He encountered no problems on his pilgrimage—at least none deriving from his assumed identity. Apparently his disguise was perfect; he gained entrance not only to the cities of Medina and Mecca but into the holiest of shrines. These he described in meticulous detail, surreptitiously taking notes on scraps of paper he had concealed on his person. To this end he carried a false "Hamail," a leather pouch designed to contain a small Koran but which in Burton's case had three compartments: "one for my watch and compass, the second for ready money, and the third contained penknife, pencils, and slips of paper, which I could hold concealed in the hollow of my hand." And, in a secret pocket, he carried "a small pistol with a spring dagger, upon which dependence could be placed" (1:239). Apparently he never had to use it, though later there was a rumor spread, which Burton vehemently denied, that he had been obligated to kill a young Arab who had discovered him performing an act of nature in what the Arabs would consider an unorthodox position.

Arabian places and dangerous encounters. *Pilgrimage* contains much information of interest to the serious student of Al-Islam—its architecture, homes and public buildings, gardens, bazaars, and sacred structures which are described and measured, sketched and illustrated. But much of the attraction of these sights no doubt derives from their being "forbidden" and in the dangers attending their surreptitious describing. Intrinsically, Burton tells us, they lacked charm and were often of a disappointing drabness. In one instance, after a long and tiring march, Burton's caravan reached Bir Said (Said's Well), and he notes his disappointment with the place. The word "well" had led him to expect "a pastoral scene, wild flowers, flocks and flowing waters; so I looked with a jaundiced eye upon a deep hole full of slightly brackish water dug in a tamped hollow—a kind of punch-bowl with granite walls, upon whose grim surface a few thorns of exceeding hardihood braved the sun for a season" (1:251). And when, in Medina, he visited the "Mosque of the Prophet": "And entering the Bab-as-Rahmah—the Gate of Pity—by a diminutive flight of steps, I was astonished at the mean and tawdry appearance of a place so universally venerated in the Moslem world." Burton adds that "it suggested the resemblance of a museum of second-rate art, an old Curiosity-shop, full of ornaments that are not accessories, and decorated with pauper splendour" (1:332). And when finally in the presence of one of the greatest Moslem sanctuaries, the Kaaba, Burton admits that his feelings are quite different from those of the genuine pilgrims:

There at last it lay, the bourn of my long and weary pilgrimage, realising the fears and hopes of many a year. . . . I may truly say that of all the worshippers who clung weeping to that curtain or who pressed their beating hearts to the stone, none felt for the moment a deeper emotion than did the Haji from the far north. It was as if the poetical legends of the Arab spoke truth, and that the waving wings of angels, not the sweet breeze of the morning, were agitating and swelling the black covering of the shrine. But to confess humble truth, theirs was the feeling of religious enthusiasm, mine was the ecstasy of gratified pride. (1:160–61)

Burton gave a very complete picture of the religious ceremonies and of the city of Mecca, adding some details concerning places in the neighborhood which the earlier Burkhardt had not visited. But, as he knew, there was really very little to add to the Swiss traveler's account, and he not only paid tribute to his predecessor's accuracy, but was content merely to quote him freely. Burton was always quite willing to express his admiration for and debt to the achievements of those who went before him.

The interest of *Pilgrimage* for the general reader lies primarily in the exciting and hazardous encounters along the way, in Burton's vivid depiction of the desert and its picturesque (to the European viewer) inhabitants, the Bedouins, and in Burton's enjoyment, which he encourages the reader vicariously to share, of the daily life of the Moslem Arab.

When Burton was not describing the landscape and peoples along the way, he indulged in speculation and philosophical commentary. Crossing the desert by slow camel-train provided ample time for thought, and he reflected on the way in which human faculties are stimulated by the vast emptiness of the wastelands.

It is strange how the mind can be amused by scenery that presents so few objects to occupy it. But in such a country every slight modification of form or colour rivets observation: the senses are sharpened, and the perceptive faculties, prone to sleep over a confused mass of natural objects, act vigorously when excited by the capability of embracing each detail. Moreover, Desert views are eminently suggestive; they appeal to the Future, not to the Past: they arouse because they are by no means memorial. To the solitary wayfarer there is an interest in the Wilderness unknown to Cape seas and Alpine glaciers, and even to the rolling Prairie,—the effect of continued excitement on the mind, stimulating its powers to their pitch. (1:148)

Always aware of himself as a "civilized" European in the midst of primitive hardship, he compares his desert experience with that of life in Europe: "believe me, when once your tastes have conformed to the tranquillity of such travel, you will suffer real pain in returning to the turmoil of civilisation. You will anticipate the bustle and the confusion of artificial life, its luxuries and its false pleasures, with repugnance. Depressed in spirits, you will for a time after your return feel incapable of mental or bodily exertion. The air of cities will suffocate you, and the care-worn and cadaverous countenances of citizens will haunt you like a vision of judgement" (1:151).

Then, by way of contrast with the suffocation of civilized life in the cities, Burton reveals his joy in the excitement of his dangerous life in the desert:

Above, through a sky terrible in its stainless beauty, and the splendours of a pitiless, blinding glare, the Samun caresses you like a lion with flaming breath. Around lie drifted sand-heaps, upon which each puff of wind leaves its trace in solid waves, flayed rocks, the very skeletons of mountains, and hard unbroken plains, over which he who rides is spurred by the idea that the bursting of a water-skin, or the pricking of a camel's hoof, would be certain death of torture. . . . What can be more exciting? What more sublime? Man's heart bounds in his breast at the thought of measuring his puny force with Nature's might, and of emerging triumphant from the trial. (1:149)

It is doubtful that Burton considered his own force to be "puny." Throughout his travels he gloried in his personal strength and knowledge; he was one of those Europeans upon whom local natives gazed with wonder and awe, who actually sought out and reveled in dangers and hardships for their own sake. The desert Bedouin did not enjoy the harshness of his environment. To him a hostile nature was a fact of life, and he made himself as comfortable as possible and did not try to enhance his privations—and certainly not to deem them "sublime." But to the English explorer, the supremacy of the white race and the British Empire was beyond question. What needed to be proved was his personal mettle. Exploration and dangerous confrontations were the Englishman's modes of acquiring self-knowledge and identity; and so Burton welcomed the challenges not only of natural forces, but of other human beings who might try to cross him.

So, after traversing the Egyptian desert, he soon enjoyed a savage, but ultimately harmless, human conflict when he boarded the ship at Suez for the trip down the Red Sea. He was not traveling alone—he had picked up the colorful native entourage that would be his custom in his subsequent journeys, and they proved to be useful in physical combat. There were: Mohammed el Basyuni, a boy from Mecca whom Burton met near Suez and who was his companion and servant on the pilgrimage; Omar Effendi, a short plump Daghistani who, despite his appearance, could become quite ferocious when aroused; Hamid, a town Arab; Salih, a boy of sixteen, half Arab, half Turk, from Medina; and "Sa'ad the Demon," an African Negro, ex-slave, ex-soldier, ex-merchant, and now Omar's servant. At Suez they all boarded the *Silk el Zahab* (The golden wire) and took their places on the most desirable spot, one of the higher decks near the stern. As the ship was hopelessly overloaded, space on deck was much in demand, and soon Burton and his group were challenged by a party of wild, "insolent" pilgrims from North Africa called Maghrabis:

Our Maghrabis were fine-looking animals from the desert about Tripoli and Tunis; so savage that, but a few weeks ago, they had gazed at the cockboat, and wondered how long it would be growing to the size of the ship that was to take them to Alexandria. Most of them were sturdy young fellows, round-headed, broad-shouldered, tall and large-limbed, with frowning eyes, and voices in a perpetual roar. Their manners were rude, and their faces full of fierce contempt or insolent familiarity. A few old men were there, with countenances expressive of intense ferocity; women as savage and full of fight as men; and handsome boys with shrill voices, and hands always upon their daggers. (1:156)

Burton describes in zestful detail the free-for-all battle between the Maghrabis and his own group for possession of the choice location on the ship: "But we had the vantage-ground about four feet above them, and their palm-sticks and short daggers could do nothing against our terrible quarter-staves. In vain the *Jacquerie* tried to scale the poop and to overpower us by numbers; their courage only secured them more broken heads" (1:156–57).

This fracas, for all its surface ferocity, ended without casualties, which cannot be said of later encounters with Arab sharpshooters and bandits on the inland roads when a number of pilgrims were killed. But the ship-board battle serves largely to entertain and to present Burton in his favorite role—the fearless adventurer and hero of the hour; and also in another role, the literary man who can tell a first-rate story.

Life on the Red Sea then settled down and was disturbed only by the elements. The days were blazing with "canescent [*sic*] heat," while the nights were comparatively cold. At midday Burton wrote that "the wind reverberated by the glowing hills is like the blast of a lime-kiln. All colour melts away with the canescence from above. The sky is a dead milk-white, and the mirror-like sea so reflects the tint that you scarcely distinguish the line of the horizon. After noon the wind sleeps upon the reeking shore; there is a deep stillness; the only sound heard is the melancholy flapping of the sail. Men are not so much sleeping as half senseless; they feel as if a few more degrees of heat would be death" (1:208).

Arabian peoples and life-styles.   Burton describes with great relish an aspect of Arab life that especially attracted him. He refers to the *Kayf,* especially at times when he is feeling critical of the European life-styles and he is tired of his own restless nature:

And this is the Arab's *Kayf.* The savouring of animal existence; the passive enjoyment of mere sense; the pleasant languor, the dreamy tranquillity, the airy castle-building, which in Asia stand in lieu of the vigorous, intensive, passionate life of Europe. It is the result of a lively, impressible, excitable nature, and exquisite sensibility of nerve; it argues a facility for voluptuousness unknown to northern regions, where happiness is placed in the exertion of mental and physical powers; where *Ernst is das Leben;* where niggard earth commands ceaseless sweat of face, and damp chill air demands perpetual excitement, exercise, or change, or adventure, or dispassion, for want of something better. In the East man wants but rest and shade: upon the banks of a bubbling stream or under the cool shelter of a perfumed tree, he is perfectly happy, smoking a pipe, or sipping a cup of coffee or drinking a glass of sherbet, but above all things deranging body and mind as little as possible; the trouble of conversations, the displeasures of memory, and the vanity of thought being the most unpleasant interruptions to his *Kayf*. No wonder that "Kayf" is a word untranslatable in our mother tongue. (1:9)[4]

While Burton was interested in the Moslem cities and shrines, it was the people of the desert that most fascinated him. His predecessor Burkhardt had not given physical descriptions of the Bedouin—the "racial portrait" which was a constant feature in Burton's travel writings. Burton's account of the physiognomies of the desert race was spiced, as usual, with references to sexual habits, virility rites, and marriage customs that emphasized the frequency of inbreeding. When dealing with such material his footnotes often appeared in Latin, and where this was not considered a sufficient protection for Victorian sensibilities, Burton resorted to Greek. He describes the "Badawin of Al-Hijaz" in his customary sharp detail, carefully cataloging every feature and trait, from stature to hair, eyes, ears, neck, shins, buttocks, and even thumbs, which he likened to those of the Celt. Always attentive to the woman, he says, "her eyes are fierce, her features harsh and her face haggard; like all people of the south, she soon fades, and in old age her appearance is truly witch-like. Withered crones abound in the camps, where old men are rarely seen" (2:85)—evidence of the rigor and harshness of the Bedouin life.

In general, Burton has praise for the Bedouin's character and manners, and he compares them to the American Indians. What is interesting in this portrayal is the presence in the picture of the author himself. In depicting those "noble savages" he is to large extent depicting himself: the Bedouin's wild chivalry, his fiery sense of honor, his taste for the blood feud and the vendetta, his gravity and caution in demeanor, social formality, and love of plundering when carried out according to the strict rules of the desert. (We would have to exempt Burton from "cautious" demeanor.) He sees these Arabs as powerfully eloquent, dry of humor, satirical and whimsical, ironic, fond of boasting and spouting pithy proverbs, and speaking in languages "wondrous in their complexity." Here is a race Burton could genuinely admire and identify with.

At other times, however, and in other moods, Burton describes the desert Arabs in less admiring terms, for it was primarily the Bedouins who made a practice of ambushing pilgrim caravans. Burton tells how, on one occasion, the caravan found itself approaching Shaub Al-Haji ("Pilgrim Pass"). A silence fell over the party as it knew it was about to enter a natural ambush; and sure enough, soon puffs of smoke could be seen curling up from the rocky hillside above them, followed by the crack of the Bedouins' matchlock guns. A number of Arabs were seen "swarming like hornets over the crests of the hills." These Bedouin "bandits" did not appear to gain much loot from their attacks but they had a grand time shooting at the pilgrims. By the time the caravan made it through the pass they left behind twelve dead men and a number of camels and donkeys.

Burton and T. E. Lawrence: a comparison.   Many years after the publication of *Pilgrimage,* a scholar questioned T. E. Lawrence about the accuracy of Burton's book. Lawrence described it as "absolutely correct in every detail" and "a most remarkable work of the highest value to a geographer or to a student of the East."[5] It can be added that *Pilgrimage* also has value for the general reader who will find it to be a grand adventure story, interlarded, as always in Burton's travel books, with scholarly information (which the reader may skip, of course).

Seen sometimes as "rivals" in their portraits of Arab life, Burton's *Pilgrimage* and Lawrence's *Seven Pillars of Wisdom* (1926) have often invited comparison. Their authors obviously had much in common: they were both scholars as well as soldiers and adventurers. They both had lived as Arabs and experienced deeply the Islamic life and culture, and they had an equal interest in describing landscapes and peoples. But the differences between the two men and the two books are equally apparent: Lawrence tends to be more gentle, introspective, lyrical; Burton is more detached, tough-minded, dramatic, at times harsh. While Burton is very much "on stage" in his narratives, he is there as an actor, wearing one of his disguises; Lawrence gives a sustained and revealing self-portrait, intimate, and confessional. He illuminates himself, whereas Burton conceals his true self, and illuminates the Arab world around him. Burton consistently shows his passion for fact-collecting on a large scale; Lawrence is more personal and selective in his choice of subjects for description.

For both men the attraction of the Arab world was essentially its "masculinity." As Burton said, "El Islam seem purposely to have loosened the ties between the sexes in order to strengthen the bonds which connect man and man."[6] But Burton admired the Arab women and found them for the most part very attractive, whereas Lawrence, who was apparently not interested in the opposite sex in any form, expresses his horror at what he considers the uncleanliness of Arab females, especially when compared with the "clean bodies" of Arab boys. Burton, who intimates that he had affairs with Eastern women, frequently defines the charms of the desert maidens and expresses respect for their strength of character: "I have often lain awake for hours listening to the conversation of the Bedouin girls, whose accents sounded in my ears rather like music" (he will say the same thing about the lyrical voices of the African Somali girls); and he points out that the "weaker sex . . . in troubled times . . . remedying its great want, power, raises itself by courage, physical as well as moral."[7]

As a literary stylist, Lawrence seems to have gathered more praise than has Burton. Both men wrote masterpieces of travel literature, but the quality of Lawrence's style, in the view of many critics, is more sustained, his portrait of the Islamic world more consistent, whereas Burton was more erratic in his judgments, uneven in literary quality, and occasionally self-contradictory in his depiction of the Arab peoples. The reasons for these inconsistencies, which are found in all of Burton's travel books, will be explored more fully in our final chapter.

Chapter Four
The African Adventures: East Africa

Some of Burton's most readable and entertaining, as well as controversial, books resulted from his adventures in the "Dark Continent." In these works we see the seasoned traveler, with his explorations of India and Arabia behind him but still pursuing the by-ways of Islamic culture, as he found them in diluted forms in East Africa, and encountering for the first time races and cultures which he will find entirely alien—those of Black Africa.

The First African Adventure: Somaliland and Harar

Burton began his campaign for support for the exploration of Somaliland while still in Cairo writing up his finished version of the *Pilgrimage*. After deciding against further exploration of Arabia, he had become fascinated by Africa in general and by Zanzibar in particular. Zanzibar, an island close to the east coast of Africa, had been for many years under the rule of an Arab sultan who controlled the spice and slave trade of central east Africa. On 16 November 1853 Burton wrote from Cairo to Dr. Norton Shaw, secretary of the Royal Geographical Society in London, announcing that he wished to lead a scientific expedition to Zanzibar: "It is one of the headquarters of slavery—the Americans are gently but surely carrying off the commerce of the country—and it has vast resources undeveloped. . . . You will ask why I now prefer Zanzibar to Arabia. Because I have now tried both sides of Arabia and can see no practical results. Travelling is a joy there and nothing would delight me more than leave for 3 or 4 years to the Eastern coast (of Arabia). But nothing except more discovery of deserts, valleys and tribes would come of it."[1]

Burton also tells of his meeting, while in Cairo, with a missionary, Dr. J. L. Krapf, who had lived in Ethiopia and currently reside in

Mombasa. Krapf had just arrived from Zanzibar "with discoveries about sources of the White Nile, Killamanjaro, and the Mts of the Moon which reminded one of a de Lunatica." Burton said he planned to "pump" the missionary to find out "what really has been done and want remains to be done." Burton was intrigued by Krapf's stories, and he was familiar with the writings of the eighteenth-century travelers, James Bruce and Father Lobo, who had explored parts of Abyssinia. Much of northern, southern, and eastern Africa had been penetrated, but the country of the Somali south of Ethiopia was, for good reasons, largely unknown. Thus, an expedition to Zanzibar took on added importance to Burton because it was a good point of departure for any exploration into Central Africa, and it is very probable that he had, as his ultimate objective, the discovery of the headwaters of the White Nile.

But first he must get to Zanzibar, and this he proposed to do by an indirect and partly inland route: to sail from Aden, on the south coast of the Arabian peninsula, across the Red Sea to the Somali-Arab town of Zayla. From there he would penetrate the interior of the forbidding Somali territory as far as the Moslem city of Harar and then swing south and east back to the African coast opposite the island of Zanzibar. To gather support for his project he did not return to London, but chose to sail, early in 1854, to Bombay, whence he could correspond with his chosen backers, both in London and India. In the latter group was included his friend James Grant Lumsden, senior member of the influential Bombay Council, to whom his first book on Africa, the *First Footsteps in East Africa,* would be both dedicated and addressed (throughout he refers to "my dear L"). There he filed his proposal "to penetrate via Harar and Gananah to Zanzibar" and, anticipating success despite formidable official opposition and red tape, he started lining up his fellow explorers. He chose Lieutenant William Stroyan of the Indian Navy, who had accompanied Burton on the Sind survey; Lieutenant G. E. Herne of the First Bombay Infantry; and Assistant Surgeon J. E. Stocks of the Bombay Army. Stocks died, however, before the expedition started and was replaced by Lieutenant John Hanning Speke of the Bengal Native Infantry—the man who was to figure so crucially in Burton's later African explorations. The plan, as it developed, was for Burton's three colleagues to explore individually different parts of the east coast of Somaliland, while Burton reserved for himself the dramatic penetration of Harar. They were all supposed to meet later, at a designated time, at the coastal town of Berbera.

First Footsteps in East Africa; or, An Exploration of Harar

Burton's *First Footsteps in East Africa* (1856) is a story of adventure, full of excitement, humor, philosophical speculation, and caustic commentary, and so rich in strange information that at times it becomes somewhat confusing. The style is typical: Burton jumps from personal narrative to history or geography and may, in some passages, become too technical for the average reader. But one can allow him his complicated digressions, which specialized readers will find valuable, and keep one's eyes on his main plot line, carried along by Burton's infectious zest and enjoyment in travel and discovery, and his ability, when he so chooses, to tell a good story.

Burton was also very fond of prefaces, and he customarily provided one for each of his travel books, sometimes adding new prefaces to subsequent editions. In these pages he usually offers two kinds of information: historical background material on the regions to be explored, and "editorials" in which he expresses personal opinions on previous expeditions and the state of the British Empire. In his preface to *First Footsteps in East Africa* he places his expedition in its historical context, vents his disapproval of certain British officials, and introduces his readers to the specific problems and dangers associated with the expedition about to be described.

Preparations for the penetration of Africa. In the preface to the first edition of *First Footsteps* Burton tells how, after having completed all of his business at Bombay, he went on his own to Aden, where he spent a full six months waiting for the official wheels to turn. There he put his time to good use: he studied the Somali language and interrogated the local merchants for whatever information they could give him regarding the areas he planned to explore. It was useless to ask British officials in Aden about the Somalis and their country, so he consulted the Arabs and local Somalis living in Aden, including even prostitutes, and studied whatever written reports on the area he could find.[2]

Burton explains that the British officials in Aden, far from being helpful, tried to discourage him from a venture which was far more dangerous than his pilgrimage into Arabia, since he would be traveling as a lone European and be required to have some legitimate reason for entering the "forbidden" city of Harar. "The human head once struck off does not regrow like the rose," the British informed him. They pointed out what he already knew—that no European so far had made the journey because of constant warfare among the Somali tribes and the xenophobia of the Hararis and their rulers. These warnings would be repeated by the governor of Zayla (a town on the East African coast), but Burton remained undeterred. Harar was a city which had intrigued explorers as much as had Timbuktu, the equally forbidden stronghold in the middle of the Sahara, described by Burton as "ill-famed" because Major Gordon Laing had been murdered in 1826, soon after leaving the city. Furthermore, no one even knew the correct location of Harar.

It must be borne in mind that the region traversed on this occasion was previously known only by the vague reports of native travellers. All the Abyssinian discoverers had traversed the Dankali and other northern tribes: the land of the Somal was still a *terra incognita*. Harar, moreover, had never been visited, and few are the cities of the world which in the present age, when men hurry about the earth, have not opened their gates to European adventure. The ancient metropolis of a once mighty race, the reported seat of Moslem learning, a walled city of stone houses, possessing its independent chief, its peculiar population, its unknown language, and its own coinage, the emporium of the coffee trade, the head-quarters of slavery, the birth-place of the Kat plant, and the great manufactory of cotton-cloths, amply, it appeared, deserved the trouble of exploration. That the writer was successful in his attempt, the following pages will prove. Unfortunately it was found impossible to use any instruments except a pocket compass, a watch, and a portable thermometer more remarkable for convenience than for correctness. But the way was thus paved for scientific observation. (19–20)

Without detracting in the least from Burton's achievement, we should observe that his title, *First Footsteps in East Africa,* is somewhat misleading. He, and indeed all European explorers in East Africa, followed paths established by Arab precursers and were very dependent on the Arab colonists and local Africans for assistance and guidance in their travels. But he did plan to be the first white European to gain entrance to Harar, and he puts this mission dramatically into focus in his opening paragraph:

I doubt that there are many who ignore the fact that in Eastern Africa, scarcely three hundred miles distant from Aden, there is a counterpart of ill-famed Timbuctoo in the Far West [of Africa]. The more adventuresome Abyssinian travellers, Salt and Stuart, Krapf and Isenberg, Barker and Rochet—not to mention divers Roman Catholic missioners—attempted Harar, but attempted it in vain. The bigoted ruler and barbarous people threatened death to the Infidel who ventured within their walls. . . . Of all foreigners the English were, of course, the most hated and dreaded; at Harar slavery still holds its head-quarters, and the old Dragon well knows what to expect from the hand of St. George. Thus the various travellers who appeared in beaver and black coats became persuaded that the city was inaccessible, and Europeans ceased to trouble themselves about Harar. It is, therefore, a point of honor with me, dear L, to utilize my title of Haji [honorific title given one who has made the pilgrimage to Mecca] by entering the city, visiting the ruler, and returning in safety, after breaking the guardian spell. (1:1–2)

Selection of supplies and companions. Burton begins his narrative with his departure from Aden, and from the beginning the book reads like a work of adventure fiction. He tells how, on Sunday, 29 October 1854, disguised as an Arab merchant, he sailed out of the "fiery harbour" of Aden on an Arab merchant ship bound for Africa. He was accompanied by three native servants who would be his companions on his hazardous trip, and he describes these colorful characters in detail. First, Mohammed Mahmud, usually called Al-Hammal ("the porter"), an Aden police sergeant: "a bull-necked, round-headed fellow of lymphatic temperament, with a lamp-black skin, regular features, and a pulpy figure" and possessed of the dubious traits of "prodigious inventiveness and a habit of perpetual intrigue." The second servant was Gubad, another Aden policeman, "one of those long, live skeletons, common among the Somalis: his shoulders are parallel with his ears, his ribs are straight as a mummy's, his face has not an ounce of flesh on it." The third was one Abdi Abakr, "a personage whom, from his smattering of learning and his prodigious rascality, we call the Mulla—'End of Time' "—an ironic title alluding to the prophesized corruption of the Moslem priesthood in the last epoch of the world. He is described as "a man about forty, with small, deep-set cunning eyes, placed close together, a hook nose, a thick beard, a bulging brow, scattered teeth, and a short, scant figure, remarkable only for length of back. His gait is stealthy, like a cat's, and he has a villainous grin."

Burton obviously took relish in portraying these bizarre travelers, but why he chose them is not made clear, since to a large extent the success of his mission, and even his life, was to depend on them. Perhaps their fantastic appearance appealed to him, as did the two burly females who were included in the entourage. Classified as cooks, they were given the names of Shahrazad and Dunyaza, after the teller of the tales, and her sister, in *The Arabian Nights*. So, while Burton's mission was exceedingly serious, he took delight in casting it, in the beginning at least, in the form of an Oriental adventure romance.

Before setting out for the interior of Africa, Burton spent twenty-six days in the coastal town of Zayla, where, he tells us, he passed his time smoking pipes, drinking coffee, and enjoying the life of a "learned Moslem." He led prayers in the mosque, read stories out loud from *The Arabian Nights*, told fortunes by palmistry, and drew out horoscopes. He argued about religion, politics, and customs, and the local citizens apparently enjoyed his company. According to Burton, they laughed at his bawdy stories, respected his physical prowess, which he was never reluctant to display, and stood in awe of his learning and the fact of his pilgrimage to Mecca. No one among the Muslims he met considered that Burton was an infidel who played a trick in doing the pilgrimage, nor did Burton look on it in this light. In such company he was a "true Moslem" and there were those who argued that Burton professed to be a Moslem up to the day of his death. He also studied Somali weapons and tactics, and impressed the local natives with his own considerable prowess with the sword. He was contemptuous of the Somali spear but was to discover later, during a night attack in which lieutenant Stroyan was killed and he himself stabbed through the cheek, that the spear could be a formidable weapon in the dark.

During the days he took extensive notes on the local natives and their customs. These are described in Burton's usual style, heavy with details, learned allusions, and technical terminology, but lightened with occasional personal observations and colorful anecdotes. He portrays the physical characteristics of the Somalis and finds, as he usually does when discussing Africa, that the women are not only more attractive than their male counterparts, but stronger, more enterprising, and industrious as well.

Around the end of November 1854, Burton had obtained five camels, the two women cooks, a fourth servant, and a native guide, and was finally ready for his trip—from which nobody in Zayla who knew of the destination believed he would return alive. The local governor warned him that the path swarmed with brigands as well as warring tribes, that the Isa (Eesa) tribe had recently murdered his son, that reports had smallpox depopulating Harar, and that for a foreigner to put himself in the power of the despotic Amir of Harar meant certain death; but Burton dismissed these warnings as "oriental exaggeration." He knew, however, that African cities were prisons on a large scale "into which you enter by your own will, and leave by another's," and that in Harar there was the legend that the ruler would lose his independence and bad times descend on the city once a European had entered its sacred confines.

This did not dissuade him, any more than did the other hazards he knew he would encounter. In all of Burton's travel narratives he seems to enjoy describing vividly and dramatically the venomous snakes, scorpions and biting insects, marauding jackals and hyenas and possibly the larger nocturnal cats, a scarcity of drinkable water and decent food, and the ubiquitous fevers. He admits that he did not anticipate another major problem: thievery, loss of supplies through accidents, and desertion. Fortunately, perhaps because he was traveling comparatively light, he did not have as many of these problems as he would in his later expeditions, which would involve major caravans and major personnel problems.

Finally, after many delays and frustrations, the party left Zayla. As it turned out, the heat was so oppressive they traveled only in the early morning and evening hours. After several days of walking through a bleak land inhabited largely by the anticipated brigands whom Burton's group managed to avoid, they reached a more populous region with numerous villages affording a modicum of hospitality and information to the explorers—for a price, that is, as bribes and other "transit fees" were an understood part of traveling in this country.

As happens on most all of Burton's African journeys, he became ill, due largely, he explains, to bad food, worse water, and temperature changes ranging from 107° at midday to 51° at night. Mere illness, however, never impeded a Burton party, so they continued their slow progress, with Burton taking his voluminous notes on everything that came to his attention: local geography, agriculture, weather, animal life, possible mineral holdings, and, above all, on the Somali inhabitants, their physical appearance, social and sexual predilections, and tribal customs, drawing interesting distinctions between the various tribes and racial types he encountered. These descriptions, vividly detailed and often accompanied by Burton's own drawings, offer, especially for their time, a rare firsthand picture of the inhabitants of Somaliland and Abyssinia. Also, they reveal Burton's inability to portray African people without strong bias, derision, and contempt.

Descriptions of the African peoples.   When writing his books, Burton's usual procedure, in dealing with an African tribe, is first to discuss it from a historical and "racial" standpoint. For example, he explains that "The Somal, by their own traditions as well as their strongly-marked physical peculiarities, their customs, and their geographical position, may be determined to be a half-caste tribe, and off-shoot of the great Galla race," and are now "a mixture of Egyptian, Negro, and Caucasian races from the East." He will then proceed to these "strongly-marked peculiarities" in his physical descriptions, where he will usually reveal his anti-Negro bias. After commending the "beauty of the brow" of the average Somali, the "large and well-formed eyes," "frequently handsome and expressive," he will point out that the appearance is "marred" by the jaw, almost invariably "prognathous and African," and by the broad, turned-out lips which "betray approximation to the Negro." The chin "projects to the detriment of the facial angle": "In mind the Somal are as peculiar as in body. They are a people of most susceptible character, and withal uncommonly hard to please. . . . They have all the levity and instability of the Negro character: light minded as the Abyssinians . . . they pass without any apparent transition into a state of fury, when they are capable of terrible atrocities" (2:77–78).

Burton's observations on the East African native were not, however, entirely negative. One thing he did admire in the Somalis was the female, especially her voice, which he found to be soft, low, and rather plaintive, pleasant to listen to. He commends the women in other ways as well: "In muscular strength and endurance the women of the Somal are far superior to their lords: at home they are engaged all day in domestic affairs, and tending to the cattle; on journeys their manifold duties are to load and drive the camels, to look after the ropes, and, if necessary, to make them; to pitch the hut, to bring water and firewood, and to cook." In the matter of drink, both sexes are "equally temperate from necessity." The mead and beer drunk by other Africans, often to excess, are unknown to the Somali of the plains. Nevertheless, "As regards their morals, I regret to say that the traveller does not find in them the golden state which Teetotal doctrines lead him to expect. After much wandering, we are almost tempted to believe the bad doctrine that morality is a matter of geography; that nations and races have, like individuals, a pet vice, and that by restraining one you only exasperate another. As a general rule, Somali women prefer *amourettes* with strangers, following the well-known Arab proverb, 'The newcomer filleth the eye.' " But he adds, "generally, the Somali women are of cold temperament, the result of artificial as well as natural causes."[3]

One of the redeeming features of Somali culture in Burton's eyes, no doubt, was their religion, which was Islamic but "tainted" with a "diversity of superstitions attesting to their pagan origin. Such, for instance, are their oaths by stones, their reverence of cairns and holy trees, and their ordeals of fire and water." After observing that in this respect the Somali are not very different from Europeans of a few centuries earlier, Burton adds: "Though superstitious, the Somal are not bigoted like the Arabs. . . . Nominal Mohammedans, Al-Islam hangs so lightly upon them, that apparently they care little for making it binding upon others." Elsewhere Burton will have sour remarks to make concerning the Christian passion for conversion.

Another of the traits Burton admired was the Somali eloquence: "The Somali language is no longer unknown in Europe. It is strange that a dialect which has no written character should so abound in poetry and eloquence. There are thousands of songs, some local, others general, upon all conceivable subjects, such as camel loading, drawing water, and elephant hunting; every man of education knows a variety of them" (2:80–81). In offering this compliment, Burton is departing from his general view, reinforced especially by his later experiences among the West Africans, that the African race is notably deficient in the development of the arts.

Burton reserves his most caustic comments for the Somali's savagery in battle and lack of personal honor: "As regards courage, they are no exception to the generality of savage races. . . . In their great battles a score is considered a heavy loss; usually they will run after the fall of a half a dozen. . . . The bravest will shirk fighting if he has forgotten his shield: the sight of a lion and the sound of a gun elicit screams of terror. . . . Yet they are by no means deficient in the wily valour of wild men: two or three will murder a sleeper bravely enough; and when the passions of rival tribes, between whom there has been a blood feud for ages, are violently excited, they will use with asperity the dagger and spear. Their massacres are fearful." He describes how one tribe, having left their women and children, the sick and aged, in their camp while they carried on their trading business elsewhere, returned to find that a foraging party of Isas had attacked the camp and old men, women, and children had been indiscriminately put to the spear (2:78–79).

The forbidden city of Harar.   Burton's technique in writing his travel books is to interweave the narrative of exploration with his anthropological observations. In these changes of focus Burton's persona shifts from that of the note-taking researcher to that of the storyteller who relates, in an almost novelistic style, his dramatic adventures. Thus when he is not examining the Somali culture and peoples in detail, he picks up on his narrative of the daring attempt to penetrate the city of Harar.

He tells how on 27 December (Christmas had not amounted to much that year), he entered the village of the chief of the area that included Harar. While the walled city itself was not included in the chief's jurisdiction, his support was necessary in making the proper approach to the city. Burton was well received, and after submitting to the required ritual ceremonies which did little to soothe a persistant stomach disorder, he rested a few days and then set forth, in the company of his three companions, Al-Hammal, the "gaunt Gulad," and "End of Time," to complete the last leg of the journey. Here Burton was confronted by an extremely important decision: up to now he had worn Arab clothing and affected Moslem manners, but he had neglected to darken his face with the customary walnut juice. He decided to abandon his attempts at disguise, which had served him so well in the past, and to enter Harar boldly as an Englishman. He gives two reasons for this decision: "All the races amongst whom my travels lay, hold him nidering [base, cowardly] who hides his origin in places of danger; and secondly, my white face had converted me into a Turk, a nation more hated and suspected than any European, without our prestige."[4] The first reason certainly did not figure in his Arabian adventures and so it is probably the second which was the valid one. As an excuse for his intrusion into the forbidden city, he forged a letter purporting to be from the political agent in Aden to the Amir of Harar, with instructions for Burton to deliver it in person. The ostensible objective was to open up better relations between the two cultures.

At this change of tactics "End of Time" was overcome with terror and had to be left behind, so Burton went to Harar accompanied only by the gaunt Gulad and Al-Hammal, with two local tribesmen as an escort. In a few hours their eyes rested on the long-sought prize, the fabled city, and it was something of a disappointment. The momentous occasion, however, was not lost on Burton: "About two miles distant on the crest of a hill, stood the city—end of my present travel—a long, somber line, strikingly contrasting with the white-washed towns of the East. The spectacle, materially speaking, was a disappointment: nothing conspicuous appeared but two grey minarets of rude shape: many would have grudged exposing three lives to win so paltry a prize. But of all that have attempted, none have ever succeeded in entering that pile of stones: the thorough-bred traveller, dear L., will understand my exultation, although my two companions exchanged glances of wonder" (1:201).

There follows one of the more interesting chapters in Burton's book, "Ten Days at Harrar," which avoids technical description in favor of dramatic narration. He conveys effectively the sense of uniqueness and danger of his situation, and keeps himself front and center of his exciting adventure. He tells how, after a half-hour's wait at the city's gate, his party was granted admission, whereupon Burton rather surprisingly embarked upon a series of defiant gestures that might have brought trouble. When told he must not walk to the Amir's palace but must trot at a rapid pace, he flatly refused, and proceeded to stroll along in a leisurely fashion. Then, after squatting in a courtyard for a half hour, in company with other supplicants for an audience with the Amir, Burton engaged in an altercation with the guard who came to escort him into the royal chambers: "Then ensued a long dispute, in tongues mutually unintelligible, about giving up our weapons: by dint of obstinacy we retained our daggers and my revolver. The guard raised a door curtain, suggested a bow, and I stood in the presence of the dreaded chief." He, too, offered an unexpected aspect: "The Amir, or as he styled himself, the Sultan Ahmad bin Sultan Abu Bakr, sat in a dark room with white-washed walls, to which hung—significant decorations—rusty matchlocks and polished fetters. His appearance was that of a little Indian Rajah, an etiolated youth twenty-four or twenty-five years old, plain and thin-bearded, with a yellow complexion, wrinkled brow and protruding eyes. His dress was a flowing robe of crimson cloth, edged with snowy fur, and a narrow white turband tightly twisted around a tall conical cap of red velvet. . . . Being an invalid he rested his elbow upon a pillow, under which appeared the hilt of a Cutch sabre" (1:206).

Burton entered the room with a confident "Peace be with you" in Arabic, to which the Amir replied graciously, extending a hand "boney and yellow as a kite's claw" and snapping his fingers. The guest was expected to kiss the hand on both sides, but Burton did not comply, "being naturally averse to performing that operation upon any but a woman's hand." No offense was taken, apparently, and the Amir proceeded to ask the nature of Burton's errand. The Amir listened with a "frowning brow" as Burton presented his fraudulent letter and explained, in Arabic, his important mission, concluding with an allusion to the friendship formerly existing between the English and the Amir's father, the deceased Sultan Abu Bakr. At this the Amir "smiled graciously," and Burton admits that smile was an enormous relief. He had been prepared for the worst, and "the aspect of affairs in the palace was by no means reassuring" (1:207).

Thus the first interview went off well enough, and Burton and his party were assigned to quarters of the Amir's "second palace" where they were fed regally on a "dish of Shabta, holcus cakes soaked in sour milk, and thickly powdered with red peppers." Beds were provided and the exhausted guests collapsed gratefully. On that first night Burton reflected: "I was under the roof of a bigoted prince whose least word was death; amongst a people who detested foreigners; the only European that had ever passed over their inhospitable threshold, and the fatal instrument of their future downfall" (1:209).

Burton sustains the story's suspense when he relates how, at one of the subsequent interviews with the Amir, he introduced a delicate topic that was beginning to concern him: when would the Amir give him a response to take back to Aden and permit him to depart in peace? Burton offered, as reason for an early reply, the information that his health was adversely affected by Harar's high, dry air and that his companions were worried about the smallpox then sweeping through the city. The Amir indicated that he would give an answer, but did not say when. So, having expended considerable effort getting into Harar, Burton now began to devote his time to the business of getting out. He even tried to enlist the support of the local chief in this endeavor. To attempt an escape without official permission would have been suicide.

While he was waiting, Burton, as he always did, put his time to good use in examining the town and its inhabitants, and assembling a glossary of Harari words and expressions (which he would publish as an appendix to his book). But he was so closely watched at every moment that he found it almost, but not quite, impossible to make his usual notes and sketches. He could never relax for a second, for while he was apparently free to wander as he pleased, he knew that he was under surveillance and that one false step, whatever that might be, could prove fatal. It was the most threatening position he had ever been in. Nevertheless, he succeeded in getting his materials, for his book is rich in recorded detail and several drawings of Harari men and women in their native costumes.

Departure from Harar and return to the coast. The day finally came (the visit was only of ten days' duration but seemed infinitely longer) when he was summoned into the presence of the Amir, given a letter to deliver to officials in Aden (along with a request that Burton arrange to send a "Frank" physician to attend the ailing Amir), and granted permission to leave the city. Thus, after the usual delays because of weather and improper days for beginning journeys (for religious reasons), mules were loaded and Burton's party began, on 13 January 1855, to retrace its path to the coast. One more hazardous experience awaited them, one as fraught with danger, in its way, as the visit to Harar. They had to cross a formidable expanse of desert with scanty supplies (a few limes, five biscuits, some sugar) and only one bottle of water among the four of them—Burton and his original three servants, "End of Time" having now rejoined the group. The others, including the two women cooks, had been sent back in a different caravan. Burton had decided on a short-cut which was not a regular caravan route, and he knew that any accident to his mules or to the one water bottle would mean a terrible death for all of them. He vividly describes his desperate five-day march across the desert area:

The demon of Thirst rode like Care behind us—for twenty-four hours we did not taste water, the sun parched our brains, the mirage mocked us at every turn, and the effect was a species of monomania. As I jogged with eyes closed against the fiery air, no image unconnected with the want suggested itself. Water ever lay before me, water lying in the shady well, water in streams bubbling icy from the rock, water in pellucid lakes inviting me to plunge and revel in its treasures. . . . I opened my eyes to a heat-reeking plain, and a sky of that eternal metallic blue so lovely to painter and poet, so blank and death-like to us. . . . I tried to talk— it was in vain; to sing—in vain; vainly to think, every idea was bound up in one subject—water. (2:57)

It is said that twenty-four to thirty hours without water on a sun-baked desert are usually enough to kill a man, yet Burton and his companions went thirty-six hours without water. They were in despair and near collapse when Burton spied, through bleary eyes, a sand-grouse fly overhead and land a short distance away. Knowing that the sand-grouse often sought water in the evening, Burton followed to the bird's landing place and found a small life-saving spring. He says he never again shot a sand-grouse.

Burton's narrative ends on 31 January 1855 when his party reached the coastal town of Berbera and joined his friends, Speke, Herne, and Stroyan. Exhausted, Burton fell into his first secure sleep in weeks, "conscious of having performed a feat which, like a certain rider to York, will live in local annals for many and many a year." But, as one recent scholar has put it, "today, as far as can be determined, no one remembers."[5]

Burton's Divided View of the Somalis

One of Burton's tendencies, when writing his books on Africa, is to be inconsistent. He reserves the right to change his mind, even to contradict himself, and sometimes the opinions he expresses in his books are not those he includes in his official government reports. However, when considering Burton's usually contemptuous comments regarding the African people, one should bear in mind that they were often the expressions of his feelings of the moment, when he was understandably not in the best of moods, suffering as he did from physical hardships and illnesses as well as frustrations and exasperations at the endless irritating complications of dealing with the local Africans. His experiences, as he related them, would indeed try the patience of a saint, and he wrote his popular books immediately upon his emerging from the jungles, straight from his notes, without distancing his experiences.

When Burton did distance his feelings a bit, as he apparently did in his official reports to government agencies, he allowed himself more favorable views of the Somalis. On his way from Zayla to Harar, for example, he was pleasantly surprised to find Somalis who had traveled widely through Arabia, India, and Egypt: "Many speak with fluency three or four languages and are perfectly acquainted with English manners and customs." He even found some commendable traits of character: "They [the Somalis] evince a great gentleness of disposition and a docility which offer fair hopes to civilisation in this region of barbarism . . . people, who in my humble opinion, are capable of being raised high in the scale of humanity. . . . Every free-born man holds himself equal to his ruler, and allows no royalties or prerogatives to abridge his birth-right of liberty. Yet I have observed, that with all their passion for independence, the Somal, when subject to strict rule as at Zayla and Harar, are both apt to discipline and subservient to command." Here Burton is speaking of the Somali in general, not of the "traitorous Isas." These views on the Somali capacities as soldiers obviously contradict statements found in his *First Footsteps,* and they are corroborated by more recent students of East Africa.[6]

Burton also had some advice to give the European governments: he pointed out that, despite their appearance of lawlessness, the Somalis had a well-balanced and intricate society. He warned against any European intervention or meddling in Somali affairs, stating that "our partial intervention" into matters in Zayla and Berbera "has been fraught with evils to them, and consequently to us."[7]

Here Burton is reversing his views on the operations of the British Empire, at least as regards Africa. In his 1856 preface to *First Footsteps,* after describing the great days of explorations along the Somali coast, the Red Sea, Persian Gulf, and the coastal areas of southern Arabia, Burton praised the work of Vice-Admiral Sir Charles Malcolm, under whose charge "the British name rose high in the Indian, African, and Arabian seas." He then sharply criticizes Malcolm's successor, Sir Robert Oliver, as "a violent, limited, and prejudiced man" under whose control "the Indian navy was crushed by neglect and routine into a mere transport service." Burton urges a return to the military power of the earlier years, insisting that only strength is understood by the native rulers and that only force creates and maintains colonial empires. In a strong statement in favor of an aggressive policy, Burton makes clear his wholehearted support for British imperialism in the East. In these assertions he was willing to make enemies of some high officials, while convincing others that his projected expeditions, for which he requested financial and diplomatic support, would further the cause of British military and economic dominion.

In his later books on Africa, however, Burton greatly modifies these views, for, by the middle 1860s, he had become surprisingly anti-imperialist. After spending several years on the African continent and seeing firsthand the effects of British colonialism, he urged the British government not only to keep its hands out of East African affairs but also to abandon its consulateships at Badagri, Lagos, and Palma on the west coast. But first, before he would be ready for such assertions, Burton had several more explorations to make and more books to write, of which the next would be *The Lake Regions of Central Africa*.

The Second African Adventure

During the mid-nineteenth century several events occurred which influenced Burton to explore East and Central Africa and to write his book on *The Lake Regions of Central Africa*. Three German missionaries working out of Mombasa (on the east coast) had provoked considerable interest and speculation by the production of a tentative map of the interior of East Africa. They had traveled extensively in those remote regions and their map showed some remarkable features, including snow-covered peaks of Mount Kenya and Mount Kilimanjaro. Many geographers were skeptical, claiming it was impossible for snow to be found on the equator, even at mountainous heights. Surely, they argued, the good fathers had mistaken the sun reflecting off light-colored rocks for the presence of snow. The missionaries also had talked with Arab merchants who had traveled much further into the interior and had reportedly seen a great inland sea, which they called "Sea of Ujiji" or "Sea of Tanganyika."[8] These controversial reports naturally stirred Burton's imagination, and he resolved to travel to the "inland sea," to determine its true location and size, if indeed it existed, to study the ethnography of tribes in the vicinity, and to gather information on the trade and produce of the region. In stating these objectives, for which he gained financial support from the Royal Geographical Society and the Foreign Office, Burton intentionally avoided mentioning the headwaters of the Nile. As he explains, "In these days every explorer of Central Africa is supposed to have set out in quest of the coy sources of the White Nile, and when he returns without them, his exploration, whatever may have been its value, is determined to be a failure" (1:5).

The Lake Regions of Central Africa: A Picture of Exploration

The Lake Regions (1856)[9] is, as Burton's subtitle states, a "picture of exploration," and it is written in Burton's usual manner. He begins with the problems that attend preparations for a major expedition—the delays and difficulties in assembling supplies and personnel; he then gives a vivid description of the overland trek— mostly a series of miseries and disasters, along with a few successes. Many pages are devoted to the portrayal of the local Africans and their cultures. Burton also gives a detailed account of his attempts to establish Lake Tanganyika as the source of the Nile and his subsequent bitterness when his traveling companion, John Speke, went on a side-trip and discovered the true source (as was later proved), Lake Victoria.

Burton, as always, is at the center of his narrative, coloring his descriptions with personal judgments, and praising or condemning as his mood dictates. The work is structured in Burton's characteristic manner: an alternating between "novelistic" narration, occasional technical discussions of physical aspects of the environment, and little personal essays conveying the author's opinions of the peoples and places visited. Thus the story moves rapidly when Burton is writing in his novelistic mode, and slows down markedly when Burton the scientist is at work. As with most of Burton's travel books, the reader may be inclined to skim or skip those parts of the work not to his personal taste.

Zanzibar: point of departure.   Burton and his companion, John Hanning Speke, reached Zanzibar near the end of 1856. The island had had a colorful history. The Arabs had driven out the Portuguese at the end of the seventeenth century and had established dominion over the entire East African coast, including the island of Zanzibar ruled by Sultan Majid. The Arab colonies had been scattered and disorganized until the previous sultan had taken charge; he developed the island's natural resources of cloves and other spices, and turned it into a chief center of the slave trade. By 1806, the Arab empire, ruled from the island, extended its zone of influence for 1,000 miles into the interior of the mainland, and had established trade routes and stations controlled by Arabs, who had to compete with Indian traders who had also been long established along the coastal regions. The particular road Burton planned to take—to the town of Ujiji which was supposed to be on the shores of the fabled inland sea—was under the control, more or less, of the Zanzibar sultanate, whose cooperation was essential to the success of the mission.

In the opening pages of *Lake Regions* Burton describes, with exasperation, the many complications and setbacks which resulted in his spending about six months at Zanzibar. He explored the island, the nearby coastline, and neighboring islands, and made a few short inland trips, while waiting for his plans to materialize and, possibly, for the end of the inland rainy season. He also took voluminous notes for a two-volume book on Zanzibar, which would not be published until sixteen years later.

The march to the interior: problems and disasters. The expedition finally got under way in June 1857. Much of its success was to depend on Burton's management, and in his narrative he shows himself at the center of confusion—encouraging, threatening, joking, coercing, using his knowledge of traditional caravan customs and rules to keep things going. Throughout his story he scarcely mentions Speke, and then only occasionally as "my companion."

Aside from the recurrent illnesses, the major problem encountered by the travelers was that of discipline—the trek was characterized by quarrels, theft, malingering, disobedience, laziness, drunkenness, fear, and desertion. But Burton also describes a few happy occasions—some small victories, comic scenes, joyful arrivals and departures, mutual help and comaraderie. Sometimes harsh measures were necessary, as we see in Burton's description of what was required to get the first march under way—patience plus pressure: "At length by ejecting skulkers from their huts, by dint of promises and threats, of gentleness and violence, of soft words and hard words, occasionally combined with a smart application of the *bakur*—the local 'cat' ['cat o' nine tails']—, by sitting in the sun, in fact by incessant worry and fidget from 6 A.M. till 3 P.M., the sluggish unwieldy body acquired some momentum" (1:51). If Speke was of any help, he certainly was not given any credit for it.[10]

The march to Kazeh[11] took 134 days, and was attended by extreme hardships. In addition to thefts and losses perpetrated by the porters, numerous accidents resulted in loss of materials and animals. The climate was often abominable—the same conditions as encountered on the Harar journey. Temperatures ranged from nights of biting cold to days of oppressive heat; wild beasts took their toll of pack animals if not of men; lions were often heard and rarely seen, but they and the other big cats were a constant threat; snakes were plentiful, as were jackals and some especially bold hyenas. Burton describes some men with horribly disfigured faces: it seems that sleeping out at night invited stealthy hyenas to bite a piece from the sleeping person's face and run with it.

The major sources of misery, however, which Burton depicts with as much zest as he does the sources of pleasure, were the various illnesses and voracious insects. The march took them across swamps, marshes, deserts, and stony mountain passes strewn with the bones of previous casualties. The two white men, as well as many natives, suffered continuously from malaria, dysentery, and what Burton called "marsh fever." This fever caused them to become, in Speke's case, nearly blind, and in Burton's, paralyzed in the legs. Speke had to be led and Burton carried much of the time. The brief periods of rest and recuperation were plagued by mosquitoes, tse-tse flies, and other biting insects that could pierce a canvas hammock, and by giant ants—the kind that build mounds several feet high— which attacked the campsites in droves. Burton compared their bite to the sensation of red-hot pincers—they would drive the tethered mules mad if protective measures were not taken. Burton found that the only deterrents the ants would heed were fire and boiling water. The sturdy canvas tents were helpful against most creatures but not impregnable to marauding insects. But through it all, Burton kept the party moving and his pen scribbling incessantly in his notebooks.

The helpful Arabs. As we have seen, Burton describes the Africans in striking detail, but almost always in the spirit of contemptuous criticism. In contrast, his portrait of the Arabs and their settlement at the trading station of Kazeh is sympathetic and grateful. He found the place to be a delightful oasis of comparative civilization buried deep in barbaric Africa. It was a well-established station, with solidly constructed domiciles, good food, and gracious hospitality. It was presided over by one Snay bin Amir, a well-educated Arab whose company Burton thoroughly enjoyed. Indeed, Snay was the first to give Burton firsthand information about the rumored great lake to the north of Kazeh, the "sea of Ukerewe" or the "Nyanza,"[12] and he strongly recommended to Burton that he check it out, as it was a larger lake than Tanganyika and more probably the sought-after source of the Nile; but Burton decided to stick with his original plans to investigate Tanganyika, a decision which seemed justified by the ancient geographical maps available to Burton at the time. Speke wanted to explore the Nyanza, but that venture had to wait.

Only with Snay bin Amir's help did Burton succeed in getting his caravan to move beyond Kazeh, but finally, on 19 February 1857, overcoming many more obstacles and hardships, the party gazed triumphantly on the vast waters of Lake Tanganyika—at least, all but poor Speke, whose near-blind eyes saw the lake as little more than a blue haze. He was to recover the use of his eyes, however, during their sojourn at the lake-shore town of Ujiji, whereas Burton was to remain a virtual invalid during the rest of the expedition. But Speke's physical problems were not over. One night he made the mistake of lighting a lamp in his open tent. He was immediately inundated by swarms of black beetles, one of which climbed into his ear, where it stayed and died. Speke spent weeks trying to dislodge the intruder; he suffered agonies from the resultant inflammation, and says that he nearly went mad.

Lake Tanganyika: source of the Nile?   Both men were thoroughly exhausted by the time they reached Ujiji but had their spirits raised, Burton tells us, by the local information that there was a stream of considerable size pouring out of the lake at its northern end. Burton was convinced that it would be the beginnings of the Nile, but Speke was dubious, as he had judged Tanganyika to be too low in altitude relative to the surrounding country to be the origin of such a great river. Burton, though now suffering from an ulcerated tongue, managed to arrange for boats for a trip up the lake, but it proved to be a shattering disappointment. The stream was there all right, but it flowed *into* the lake. Also, Burton was convinced by local chiefs that the lake was surrounded by high mountains to the north. So Speke's judgment of the local terrain turned out to be correct—the master surveyor proved to be as good as Burton had said he was—to Burton's everlasting chagrin and bitterness.

So Burton returned to Ujiji, where the party was stuck for a few weeks due to lost luggage which they hoped might catch up with them at Ujiji. Burton spent his time writing up his findings about Lake Tanganyika, which was after all his main charge—without completely abandoning the hope that it might after all turn out to be the source. The lost baggage finally arrived and the trip back to Kazeh began on 26 May. They reached Kazeh a month later.

Speke's success and Burton's major mistake. On the return trip Speke insisted that they should investigate Nyanza to the north, but Burton, for various reasons, declined. His legs were still in bad shape; moreover, relations between the two men, which had never been very good, had so deteriorated that Burton admitted to wanting to be rid of Speke's company for a while. He preferred to associate with his Arab acquaintances in Kazeh. Moreover, he wanted to gather as much information as possible about the country's products, commerce, and peoples of the interiors—also part of his charge.

So Burton remained in Kazeh when, on 10 July, in company with the guide Bombay and a small group, Speke headed north. He returned on 25 August with triumphant news: the reports of Lake Nyanza (which he christened Lake Victoria Nyanza) were true. He had stood on the shores and had gazed out on a lake larger than Tanganyika, and while he had not actually seen the large stream reportedly pouring out of the northern end of the lake, he had "reliable evidence." The verbal evidence he had gathered was somewhat dubious, as neither he nor his guide Bombay had a good grasp of the local languages, but Speke had other evidence. The lake was at 4,000 feet altitude, whereas that of the Nile was 2,000 feet at its southernmost charted point; he had ascertained that the rainy season at the lake was appropriate for subsequent floodings of the river to the north. This was solid evidence, but Burton only sneered and heaped derision on Speke's theories, which, as he pointed out, were based on inference and not on firsthand experience of the outflowing stream. Burton rejected the kind of evidence which he had, in fact, brought Speke along to gather.

Controversy over the source of the Nile. One can surmise that Burton's flat rejection of Speke's discovery was caused by the deep and bitter hostility that had developed between the two men. Burton's narrative makes it clear that the relationship had deteriorated to the point where Burton, apparently, was unable to cope rationally with his "companion's" success, so he very irrationally and self-destructively refused to grant Speke any credit whatsoever. And since supplies and finances were too low to permit another trip north to establish definitely whether Victoria Nyanza was the Source, the two embittered travelers headed back to the coast.

Burton's later actions, and writings, were strangely inconsistent. Though he continued to hold out against Speke's claims, and was prepared to debate the issue back in England, Burton wrote to the secretary of the Royal Geographical Society, in April 1859, urging "serious attention" for Speke's map observations and for Speke's diary of his journey to Nyanza, "as there are now reasons for thinking it to be the source or principal feeder of the White Nile."[13] Also, Burton, who was unable to compliment Speke to his face, said good things about Speke's discoveries when he returned to England— until, that is, the publication of Speke's journals in the fall of 1859 threatened his own preeminence in African exploration. Then he retaliated with public expressions of scorn at Speke's Nile theories.

Burton undoubtedly felt cheated out of the major discovery of the mid-nineteenth century, but he should not have felt that his expedition was a failure. Modern anthropologists have praised the great achievements of Burton's expedition and have commended the detailed richness of his book[14]—which indicates that he did indeed succeed in what, in the early pages of his book, he said he wanted to do: "No apology is offered for the lengthiness of the ethnological descriptions contained in the following pages. The ethnology of Africa is indeed its most interesting, if not its only interesting feature. Everything connected with the habits and customs, the moral and religious, the social and commercial state of these new races, is worthy of diligent observation, careful description, and minute illustration" (1:106). He provided a wealth of information on the Arabs and their role in East-Central Africa as well as ethnological and topographical lore of lasting value to students of black Africa. But there is also the conviction, among some recent critics as well as his contemporaries, that his writings are seriously marred by his lack of generosity toward his "companion" Speke, and by his open hostility toward and contempt for the African black. Despite the many virtues of *The Lake Regions,* the contempt at times seems ludicrous. The impulse to write and publish superficial opinions and Burton's indulgence in derision frequently seem to have mastered him and spoiled much that was otherwise of great value.

Zanzibar: City, Island, and Coast

In *Zanzibar* (1872)[15] Burton describes in vivid detail many aspects of the fabulous island that came to his attention. But before turning to the island itself, he devotes a chapter to matters which he usually reserved for his prefaces: his grievances. In this case he complains of the money which he and Speke had spent, many years earlier, on their Somaliland adventures, "without redress" from the various authorities to whom they had applied; and he showed that he was still smarting under the criticism received as a result of a night attack during which Lieutenant Stroyan had been killed. Since this book was published sixteen years after being written, the first chapter also refers to his subsequent work, *The Lake Regions of Central Africa*.

The narrative follows Burton's usual method: a weaving back and forth between personal anecdote—"Arrival at Zanzibar Island" and "A Stroll through Zanzibar City"—and carefully gathered scientific data—"Notes on the Fauna and Flora of Zanzibar," "The Ethnology of Zanzibar," "Thermometric Observation in East Africa," and the like. He poked into all parts of the city, including the prison where he saw the prize prisoner: "a poor devil cateran who had beaten the death-drum whilst his headman was torturing M. Maizan." The unfortunate Lieutenant Maizan, a twenty-six-year-old French naval officer, had been the last European to attempt an inland march from the East African coast. He had been taken prisoner by Mazungera tribesmen and ritually executed in a horrible fashion—which no doubt gave Burton something to think about, since he and Speke were to be the next Europeans in that area. But Burton also found other less gruesome sights to report. He recounted the history of the island and its mixture of peoples, compiled meteorological data, made notes on the local animal and vegetable life, collected local proverbs, and took a strong interest in the lives of the Zanzibaris. He noted that doctors did not seem to exist, whereas disease was rampant. Urinary and genital diseases were everywhere: "gonorrhoea is so common that it is hardly considered a disease." He also noted with some satisfaction that "in these lands a drunkard outlives a water-drinker." He found few prostitutes on Zanzibar, perhaps because of the prevalence of slave-girls; he noted that white slave-girls were rare, and that most white residents kept Abyssinian or Galla concubines. He describes the Negro population in his usual prejudiced way, seeing them as "an undeveloped and not to be developed race," and commenting acidly on "Negro insolence." Even the Arabs, whom Burton usually praised, he found to be a debased element on the island: "wealth has done much to degenerate the breed, climate more, and slavery most." Indolence had resulted in "luxury and unbridled licentiousness."

Zanzibar is an interesting book for the general reader, though somewhat disillusioning. The aura of Eastern romance that once hovered about the name "Zanzibar" is thoroughly dispelled by Burton's grim depiction of rampant sordidness and misery.

Chapter Five

Travels in West Africa and North America

Exploring West Africa

When, in 1861, Burton traveled to his first consular post, he was not in the best frame of mind. He had failed to obtain the position he had long cherished—the consulate at Damascus—and found himself, instead, shipped off to the unhealthy and unpopular island of Fernando Po off the west coast of Africa. It was doubtless galling to Burton, now forty years old, a celebrity and the author of famous books on East Africa and the Near East, to be relegated to the lowest rung of the diplomatic ladder among the black natives he had come to despise. However, he performed the minimum of required consular work and devoted the rest of his time to exploration and writing. He was on his island only a week before he was off examining the delta of the Niger. He returned to Fernando Po only to use it as a staging-ground for his next expedition—to Abeokuta, the capital of Nigeria, where he stayed for three weeks. Then he explored the Brass and Bony rivers, and, a month later, took off for southern Nigeria to climb the highest peaks of the Cameroons Mountains. Then, in February of 1862, he went up the Gabon River in quest of gorillas and cannibals. Later that year, after a four-month leave in England, he returned to Africa to carry out his most publicized expedition, the trip to Dahomey, the African kingdom notorious for its mass human sacrifices and Amazon army.

During these three years (1861–63) Burton took great quantities of notes which he transformed into four two-volume books of travel and one extensive compilation of native proverbs. The latter, *Wit and Wisdom in West Africa* (1865), is an uncharacteristic tribute to native sagacity and verbal felicity, but the travel books, *Wanderings in West Africa* (1863), *Abeokuta and the Cameroons Mountains* (1863), *Two Trips to Gorilla Land and the Cataracts of the Congo* (1876), and

A Mission to Gelele, King of Dahome (1864) can be justly described as studies in disenchantment.

Wanderings in West Africa, From Liverpool to Fernando Po

Wanderings in West Africa (1865)[1] is Burton's journal of his trip from England to Fernando Po. His ship made frequent but brief stops at well-known islands and port towns along the West African coast, and Burton was determined, as he put it in his preface, "to lay down what a tolerably active voyager can see and do during the few hours allowed to him by the halts of the mail packet." And so he gives us his detailed impressions of "a day at Madeira," a day each at the islands of Tenerife and St. Mary's, "Three Days at Freetown, Sierra Leone," and "Six Hours at the Cape of Cocoa Palms," using the occasions to air his attitudes and opinions on any topic that came to his mind. The narrative is presented in a rather slap-dash manner, which Burton hopes his readers will forgive: "amidst an abundance of greater there is doubtless a crowd of minor blemishes, which those charitably disposed will attribute to the effects of a 'single revise.' "

While Burton rarely apologizes for expressing opinions about strange places on brief acquaintance, here he justifies his methods in a way that applies equally to his other travel books: "Despise not, gentle reader, first impressions, especially in a traveller. . . . I am convinced . . . that if a sharp, well-defined outline is to be drawn, it must be done immediately after arrival at a place; when the sense of contrast is still fresh upon the mind, and before second and third have ousted first thoughts. . . . The man who has dwelt a score of years in a place, has forgotten every feeling with which he first sighted it" (20–21). The book is dedicated to "The True Friends of Africa—not to the 'philanthropists' or to Exeter Hall," and he gives as the author "F.R.G.S." (Fellow of the Royal Geographical Society). One wonders about this emphasis on credentials rather than on name, but perhaps it spurred Burton to an even greater freedom of expression than he enjoyed in his other books, candid as they were, for he offers opinions and prejudices unrestrained. He offers pithy comments on the "philanthropists," along with Jews, Americans, Irishmen, Negroes, and missionaries, having little good to say about any of them. He also discusses sharks, narcotics, slavery, cannibalism, tse-tse flies, gold mining, circumcision, remedies for tropical diseases, legal punishments, aphrodisiacs, mulattos, colonial salaries, geographical exploration, port management, and finally, Negro education and Negroes in "white man's clothing"—both of which he deplores.

Most readers probably become inured to Burton's habitual acerbity, accept his barbs as inevitable Burtonisms, and find value in the wealth of commentary on intrinsically interesting topics. His invective is "democratic" and finds its targets in all areas: he caustically criticizes the policies and actions of most of his fellow whites in Africa, whose sole aim was fast profits. Similarly, he makes it clear that he disliked the Christian missionary almost as much as the Christianized African. He condemns the missionary for trying to replace native speech with the English language, for breaking up the polygamous marriages (Livingstone cut off from communion all natives who would not give up their extra wives), for insisting on clothing the native nakedness, and for adding to the plentitude of native fears a new fear about hell. He even accuses Jesuit missionaries of flogging their converts, and participating actively in the slave-trade. He notes sardonically that the same missionaries who objected to the native's use of "magic teeth, bones and wizard's mats," recommended in their stead "relics, medals and consecrated palm leaves." And he takes special pleasure in pointing out that in Africa evil spirits are white and ugly, as they are black and ugly in Europe.[2] Burton often takes pleasure in giving the black perspective: "The African will say, 'the white man is an old ape,' and doubt that he is human. . . . Thus we observe, that whilst the Caucasian doubts the humanity of the Hamite, the latter repays the compliment in kind."[3] And at times he drops his insistence on the inferiority of all things African. In the preface to his *Wit and Wisdom in West Africa,* which contains 2,268 native aphorisms with phonetic transcriptions from ten African tongues, he observes that many of the entries, "for brevity and elegance . . . may claim an equal rank with those of any other nation in ancient or modern times." Some examples: "Frowning and fierceness prove not manliness," "When the mouth stumbles, it is worse than the foot," "A bad person is better than an empty house."

Two Trips to Gorilla Land and
the Cataracts of the Congo

It was characteristic of Burton that he was attracted by the more sensational issues of his day—a preoccupation with cannibalism and reports of native savagery and blood thirstiness, and fearsome gorillas, which had recently captured the European imagination. Thus Burton arranged his West African explorations to take him into regions where these sinister and exciting creatures, animal and human, were supposed to be found.

Gorillas were largely unknown to Europeans and Americans before 1850, and then what was known took the form of myth and "atrocity folklore." The gorilla was considered, on the basis of scattered and unreliable reports, to be the embodiment of bestial ferocity and predatory sexuality. Tales were spread about vicious attacks on native camps, along with the abduction and rape of native women. These stories became expanded into fantasies about white women on safari being carried off into the trees by marauding great apes. This became a popular nightmare in the later nineteenth century, especially after the publication of Paul du Chaillu's *Explorations and Adventures in Equatorial Africa* (1861). Thereafter hunting the wild gorilla became fashionable, and even more wild stories began to appear. Burton knew du Chaillu, had defended him publicly against those who questioned his accounts of the apes, and he became so intrigued that he formed his own search expedition in 1862. He failed in his aim—to bring back a specimen alive—but he wrote an informative book about his attempts. *Two Trips to Gorilla Land and the Cataracts of the Congo* (1876) added little to du Chaillu's observations, except to tone them down a bit—to revise the myths about the creature's ferocity. Burton points out aspects of gorilla behavior that seem to have been corroborated by later researchers: that the gorilla is not aggressive; that his noisy bark is intended to intimidate, to drive intruders away; that he avoids battle whenever possible and prefers to be left alone. Burton states that "he is not the king of the jungle . . . the gorilla, on the seaboard at least, is essentially a coward; nor can we be surprised at his want of pluck, considering the troubles and circumstances under which he spends his harassed days" (2:251–52).

Following his disappointment at failing to capture a gorilla, Burton decided to look into the matter of cannibalism. Accordingly, he undertook an expedition far up the Gabon River to visit the Fans (or Fangs), who had a colorful reputation for cannibalism and savage cruelty. He spent less than a week among these people, and he reported them to be deceptive in their appearance. He describes them as being light-skinned, with almost Caucasian features, graceful bodies, and apparently gentle dispositions. Indeed, by Burton's standards (white European) they seemed to be a superior species. He points out that they were nevertheless an extremely dangerous and barbarous tribe whose activities had terrorized the surrounding regions. Burton discovered, however, that the reports of cannibalism, like most reports about Africans, had greatly exaggerated the facts. There was, to be sure, some eating of human flesh, the practice being confined to some private male ceremonies of a religious nature. He inquired also into the rumored practice of tanning human skins, but found that most of the hides believed to be human were made from wild cows. As in the case of the maligned gorilla, facts turned out to be less dramatic than the rumors.

Nevertheless, in other aspects the Fans proved to be as barbarous as any tribe Burton had yet encountered: "Prisoners are tortured with all the horrible barbarity of that wild human beast which is happily being extirpated, the North American Indian, and children may be seen greedily licking the blood from the ground." The Fans also murdered infant twins and buried criminals alive.[4] So while *Gorilla Land* may have dispelled or at least modified some myths about the African, it served to corroborate others, especially the African reputation for savagery.

Abeokuta and the Cameroons Mountains, An Exploration

The journey described in *Abeokuta* (1863) is in a somewhat lighter vein. Burton purported to have serious intentions in making the trip, but the main motive seems to have been pure adventure. In company with several Europeans, including a botanist, and an African guide, Burton set out to examine the fauna and flora of Nigeria, to visit the capital city of Abeokuta, and ultimately to climb the Cameroons Mountains. He gives as one of his reasons for writing the book the fact that previous accounts of the region were hopelessly inadequate, having been penned by two member of the "weaker sex"—"authoresses, who are not travellers, have produced neat little drawing-room sketches, all *couleur de rose.*" (He does not name the books.) Two other books had been written "in the missionary-African line; they, of course, run in a well-known grove" (1:vi). Thus there remained much to be said about Abeokuta and environs.

Burton's story is told in relatively high spirits, with humorous episodes and some self-directed humor. He describes his altercations with the riverboat's captain and his dog, toward both of which Burton felt a deep antipathy. The dog, he tells us, "was a most amiable animal; when tied up, he barked and howled most musically all the way, and when loose he insisted upon springing overboard, stopping the boat, and exciting different emotions amongst those in it. A St. Helena pointer—he even pointed at butterflies—and he was just recovering from mange." When the animal was lost overboard, Burton observed, "Of course we made on the way down all inquiries for so pleasant a companion, but we had to mourn his loss." Burton also describes his mishaps with horses on consecutive "unlucky" Fridays, and concludes that he was fortunate to have survived his encounters with "a wild beast of Yoruba pony" (1:63, 84).

Burton makes fun of the local missionaries in his usual way, and chastises them, in all seriousness, for having dragged their poor wives out to such barbarous places. He found much less to criticize among the African tribes, who showed the travelers much hospitality. The natives gave parties for them, with singing, feasting, and dancing. Burton describes the women as attractive, with fine figures: "Our hosts were perfectly civil and obliging, and so were our hostesses—rather too much so I could prove, if privileged to whisper into the reader's ear. But what would Mrs. Grundy say?" Or, more to the point, as one of Burton's biographers asks, what did Mrs. Burton say?[5] Burton, who usually found much to complain of, concluded that "upon the whole, our trip was decidedly 'jolly.' "

Thus, the Burton one does not often see in his books: lighthearted, favorably disposed, enjoying the company of Africans, writing about amusing episodes. Not amusing to his wife, obviously, who had to put up with many suggestions by her husband that he was more than a mere observer of African (and Eastern) sexual practices.

Burton devotes the last part of his book to the exploration and climbing of the Cameroons Mountains. He competed with his younger companions, both in hiking and climbing and in the collecting of rare botanical specimens, and he scaled, solo, the highest peak, leaving there a small rock cairn containing some pages of *Punch* to authenticate his achievement. He and his fellows gave names to the mountains, after the queen and Prince Albert, Isabel, Monckton Milnes and others, but the names did not stick. They were renamed, to Burton's chagrin, by later geographers.

Burton's recent biographers are convinced that he had one unpublicized reason for going to Abeokuta. It appears that he slipped over the border of neighboring Dahomey and visited the capital city of Abomey (Agbomy). He did not mention this in his writings, as he had not been granted official permission to make such a trip.[6] It was not until later, in August 1863, that Burton received authorization from the Foreign Office to visit the king of Dahomey, and he was anxious to arrive in that kingdom in time for the "ritual massacres" that were supposed to take place in celebration of the New Year.

A Mission to Gelele, King of Dahomey

The full title of Burton's book was obviously intended to capture the Victorian reader's interest: *A Mission to Gelele, King of Dahomey, With Notices of the So-Called "Amazons," the Grand Customs, the Yearly Customs, the Human Sacrifices, the Present State of the Slave Trade, and the Negro's Place in Nature* (1864).[7] The Kingdom of Dahomey was founded in 1625 and first emerged as a powerful African state in the early part of the eighteenth century. During the early nineteenth century it reached its greatest strength and influence under the rule of King Gezo (1818–58). Upon his death, his son and current ruler, Gelele, following ancient tradition, had slain 500 natives—to provide the departed king with servants in the other world—and he periodically added to that number. He also immediately began to attack neighboring states, to harass and capture Christians, and to revive the slave trade that the English and French had been striving to suppress. In the mid-nineteenth century, no kingdom in West Africa had a more sinister reputation than Dahomey. Europeans had eagerly accepted the grisly stories of 2,000 sacrificial victims with the death of every Dahoman king, and a lake of blood big enough to paddle a canoe in. While the actual number of victims did not live up to the legends, the facts, as they turned out, were shocking enough. The "yearly customs" referred to in the book's title did involve the ritual killing of large numbers of men, women, and children; and the "grand customs" carried out an even larger blood-bath on the occasion of the death of a king.

Burton gives as the official reasons that the Foreign Office decided to send him to visit King Gelele were to carry a message protesting these ritual slaughters, to try to dissuade the king from supporting the slave trade, and to gain the release of Christian prisoners taken during recent raids. Burton admits that he was personally interested in these matters, and added a motive of his own: to see for himself what the so-called Amazon army looked like. To aid in the effectiveness of his mission, he carried sumptuous gifts where-with to influence the king's decisions and reply.

The trek to the Dahoman capital.   The book gives a detailed account of Burton's trek inland and explains why it took his party weeks to make the relatively short journey to the Dahoman capital: he was obliged to sit through elaborate and lengthy ceremonies at every village and town on the route. He describes minutely the costumes, dances, food and drink (lots of rum), native characters, and the purposes served by the rituals. He also notes the countryside and found it to be a dismal sight: "The aspect of the country confirms the general impression that the Dahomans were, for Negroes, an industrious race, till demoralized by slave-hunts and by long pred-atory wars. . . . Africa, as far as I know her, shows few such ruined regions as that viewed during the last four days. The scantiness of the population, and the disproportion of women and children to adult males, strikes every age" (1:116–17). Burton later used this noticeable dearth of male adults in his discussions with King Gelele, pointing out that rather than killing off droves of men, it would be in the state's interest to keep alive as many as possible. Burton's views on this point were reinforced when, on entering the capital city, he observed many skulls posted about, nailed up on doorways and such, and dozens of prisoners bound and gagged, awaiting their fates on the appointed day.[8]

Sacrifices and atrocities.   Burton recounts how he flatly refused to have anything to do with the impending sacrifices, so the king decided, in deference to his guest's wishes, to carry out the decapitations at night, when Burton would not be present. Burton attended and describes the drawn-out presacrifice orgies, and saw dangling male corpses on the following day, all having been genitally mutilated—"in respect to the royal wives." A total of twenty-three men had been decapitated during the night, and an equal number of women, "all executed by officers of their own sex, within the palace walls, not in the presence of men." Later it appeared that eighty victims had been killed in five days, and Burton estimated that the total annual slaughter at around five hundred.

Rather than just being appalled at the bloodshed, Burton interrogated the king and other officials as to the rationale for such behavior. And in these pages Burton reveals another side of his nature. He drops his usual racist attitude and indulges in some nonmoralistic, nonethnocentric commentary that is rarely found in his books on Africa. While admitting the existence of African atrocities, he also reminds his readers of similar European practices. He recalls the guillotining of a French mother during his own childhood, and points out that Dahomey, in executing women in female privacy, "Is therefore one point more civilised than Great Britain, where they still, wondrous to relate, 'hang away' even women, in public. . . . We can hardly find fault with putting criminals to death when in the Year of Grace 1864 we hung four murderers upon the same gibbet before 100,000 gaping souls at Liverpool, when we strung up five pirates in front of Newgate, when . . . our last Christian king but one killed a starving mother of seventeen, with an infant at her breast, for lifting a yard of linen from a shop counter" (1:166–67).

Burton frequently invokes comparisons with the brutalities of European practice, often in an attempt to put African practice into perspective: "At the risk of repetition, I must again refer to the curious fixed idea in England . . . touching human sacrifice at Dahome [*sic*]. It is no mere lust of blood or delight in torture and death that underlies the rite in these lands. [The Fans, apparently, did take such delight.] The king has to perform a disagreeable task over his ancestral graves, and he does it; his subjects would deem it impious were he to curtail or to omit the performance, and suddenly to suppress it would be as if a European monarch were forcibly to abolish prayers for the dead (1:313). Furthermore, Burton quotes Gelele as saying in defense of the rituals: "he slew only malefactors and war captives who, if they could, would do the same to him; that his own subjects were never victims." The king added that the numbers had been greatly exaggerated (2:345).

In justification for the continuing slave trade, Gelele offered what Burton called a "traditional excuse": "That the slave trade was an ancestral custom established by white men, to whom he would sell all he wanted: to the English, who, after greatly encouraging the export, had lately turned against it. . . . Moreover, that the customs of his kingdom compelled him to make war, and that unless he sold he must slay his captives, which England, perhaps would like even less (2:344). Burton concludes that "of course [Gelele's] hands were tied in the case of abolishing slave export and human sacrifice, but he might have offered his minimum"—in response to England's requests.

Dahomey's "Amazon army." Burton also reports that the "Amazon army" did in fact exist. Numbering about 2,500, these women soldiers were well organized and apparently had a better fighting record than their male counterparts. They were by and large a burly bunch, many of them volunteers, but the majority were assigned to duty: "Most of them were women taken in adultery and given to the king as food for powder instead of being killed. They were mostly elderly and all of them hideous. The officers were decidedly chosen for the size of their bottoms."[9]

As Burton describes these ladies, they put on a colorful show, apparently, with their red, white, brown, and blue costumes and black horsetail headdresses. They were armed to the teeth with various old muskets and blunderbusses and all carried sharp knives of prodigious length. The women were supposed to be celibate, as befitted their martial status. In fact, as "official wives" of the king, adultery was supposed to be punished by death; yet, according to Burton, 150 were pregnant, "so difficult is chastity in the tropics."

Burton tended to disparage the Amazons' military effectiveness: "They manoeuvre with the precision of a flock of sheep. . . . An equal number of British charwomen, armed with the British broomsticks, would . . . clear them off in a very few hours," but he also admitted that in the neighboring kingdom of Abeokuta they had the reputation for being formidable fighters, capable of attacking bare-footed through thorny acacia-bush defenses, and he blamed their recent defeats on the incompetence of their male officers. While Burton generally despised the Dahomans as warriors, he gave the women their due: "I have no doubt that this physical superiority of the 'working sex,' led in the Popo and Dahoman race to the employment of women as fighters. They are the domestic servants, the ploughboys . . . and the field-hands, and market cattle of the nation—why should they not also be soldiers?" (1:111–12).

Burton's view of the Dahoman. Despite a certain show of hospitality on the part of his hosts, Burton relates that he spent most of his visit in a state of frustration and repressed fury at what he considered to be calculated delays and daily humiliations. "With characteristic Negro impudence, which ever pierces through Dahoman politeness," the king forced him to wait for six weeks for a most unsatisfactory response to the British message, and he finally departed for the coast with more than his usual contempt for the local Africans: "The modern Dahomans . . . are a mongrel breed, and a bad. They are Cretan liars, *cretins* at learning, cowardly, and therefore cruel and bloodthirsty; gamblers and therefore cheaters; brutal, noisy, boistrous, unvenerative, and disobedient, dipsa-bitten things, who deem it a 'duty to be drunk'; a 'flatulent, self-conceited herd of barbarians,' who endeavor to humiliate all those with whom they deal; in fact, a slave race—vermin with a soul apiece" (1:331).

Burton looked forward to the defeat, in an impending war, of the Dahomans by Abeokuta: "Many years must elapse before Dahome can recover from the blow, and before that time I hope to see her level with the ground" (2:364).

Burton's Portrait of the Black African

Burton observed and described, then, over a period of about ten years, a wide variety of Africans of different regions and tribes. The diversity of peoples encountered, along with Burton's own inconsistencies, do not result in a coherent portrait of "the African Negro." Burton's readers meet such diverse types as the eastern Somali, the "traitorous Isas," the friendly and hospitable tribes about Abeokuta, and "despicable Dahomans," and the terrifying Fans of gorilla land—many of them differing widely in color, features, and customs. However, while there is no common portrait, Burton does emphasize certain traits which he thought he saw in most all Africans, and those do add up to a fairly consistent, if hazy, image of the African character. In three areas especially he both drew upon, and contributed generously to the development of, a strongly negative image, or "myth," of the African Negro.

First, the nineteenth century, due in part to the Darwinian and pre-Darwinian theories of evolution, the discovery of the gorilla and of feral children, and the fascination with the "wild man" and the "missing link," was peculiarly preoccupied with primitivism and savagery, and Burton, responding to this interest, gave his readers a vivid image of the savage African. Second, he nourished the conception of the African as essentially childish, of limited intelligence, and low on the evolutionary scale with little or no capacity for development. Third, he gave considerable support to the belief in an extraordinary Negro sexuality.

Burton documents the first, the savagery and cruelty of the African, with many descriptions of gruesome native practices—ritual torture, bloody massacres, and mutilation and mass execution of enemy captives and slaves. These are described in horrifying detail and in a tone of scornful indignation—though he occasionally reminds his readers that Europeans, of a not far distant past, carried on similar practices. However, he tends to see African atrocities as evidence of generally debased and animal natures. He points out that, in Africa, "revenge is a ruling passion, as the many rancorous fraticidal wars that have prevailed between kindred clans, even for a generation, prove." He sees gross evidence everywhere that the African is indifferent to the sufferings of his fellows: "It is most painful to witness the complete inhumanity with which a porter seized with small-pox is allowed by his friends, comrades, and brethren to fall behind in the jungle, with several days' life in him."[10]

Some of Burton's critics have charged that, because of his racial bias, Burton depicted, rather selectively, only the grosser side of African character. But recent biographers have come to his defense, pointing out that much of what Burton says about Africans may sound like rabid racial hatred, but Burton was first of all an exact observer. There *was* filth, mutilation, ignorance, indolence, drunkenness, and violence. The natives did live in huts populated with "a menagerie of hens, pigeons, and rats of peculiar impudence," just like the poor in Ireland, as he was careful to point out. Certain tribes did burn their witches, again, as he noted, like Europeans of a not-too-distant date.[11]

Burton does treat his readers to many examples of hideous cruelty: "among some tribes, if a chief fell ill, the head magician tortured members of the chief's family till he either died or recovered. The women were mutilated with impalement, and many preceded their chief to the grave." Small children often suffered because of superstitious ignorance: "If an infant cut his upper incisor teeth before the lower, he was killed or sold into slavery. If twins were born, they were often both killed." However:

Among most tribes the chief cannot sell his own subjects into slavery except for two offenses: adultery and black magic. The latter crime is usually punished by the stake; in some parts of the country the roadside shows at every few miles a heap or two of ashes with a few calcined and blackened human bones with bits of half-consumed charcoal, telling the tragedy that has been enacted there. The prospect cannot be contemplated without horror; here and there, close to larger circles where the father and mother have been burnt, a smaller heap shows that some wretched child has shared their terrible fate, lest growing up he should follow in his parents' path. The power of conviction is wholly in the hands of the Mganga or medicine-man, who administers an ordeal, called Baga or Kyapo, by boiling water. If the hand after being dipped shows any sign of lesions, the offense is proven, and the sentence is instantly carried into execution. [12]

Burton emphasizes the cruel savagery of the black Africans by contrasting them with the Arabs he met in his travels. In his previous book, *The Lake Regions of Central Africa,* he recounted how, upon arriving at Kazeh, the small village serving as headquarters of a wealthy Arab merchant, he and his group were received with lavish hospitality and friendliness. Burton was delighted to be once again among "civilised" people, to drink and dine graciously and to converse in an elegant language on worthy and noble topics: "Contrary to the predictions of others, nothing could be more encouraging than the reception experienced from the Omani Arabs; striking, indeed, was the contrast between the open-handed hospitality and the hearty good-will of this truly noble race, and the niggardness of the savage and selfish African—it was heart of flesh after heart of stone." Burton always considered the Arabs to be members of a superior race, and he was apparently undisturbed by the fact that his generous Arab host had achieved his position and wealth through the corruption and exploitation of the Africans: "He had risen to be one of the wealthiest ivory and slave dealers in Eastern Africa." [13]

But while, as a rule, Burton condemned the European and Arabian countries for their part in the slave trade, which had demoralized the African and whetted his appetite for cruelty, he tended to document that cruelty, as one scholar has put it, "with an almost loving eye for detail." The extraordinary lengths he went to to expose this cruelty for all the world to shudder at probably reveals an important facet of Burton's own character. He seemed bent on searching out the worst in Africa, as if by exposing it he could exorcise his own preoccupation with cruelty.[14] It is true that he was attracted primarily to those regions noted for their "atrocity folklore."

While not accounting for his own inclinations, Burton did try to explain the cruelty of the African (and though he was speaking generally, he was thinking here of the Fans in particular): "Cruelty seems to be with him a necessary way of life, and all his highest enjoyments are connected with causing pain and inflicting death. His religious rites—a strong contrast with those of the modern Hindoo—are ever causelessly bloody. . . . I can hardly believe this abnormal cruelty to be the mere result of uncivilization; it appears to me the effect of an arrested development, which leaves to man all the ferocity of the carnivor, the unreflecting cruelty of the child."[15]

The second trait, childishness and lack of mental and moral development, Burton attributes to the Africans' remaining close to the infancy of the human race, and he sees the trait manifested not only in their cruelty but in what he considers to be their irresponsibility, dishonesty, selfish disregard for each others' welfare, lack of moral standards, and religious beliefs which he saw as being closer to primitive magic and fetishism than to the more advanced conception of a supreme being. He usually views the black as not only not evolved, but as incapable of evolving along the lines of the other races. For example, Burton begins his chapter on the character of the East African with this observation: "The study of psychology in East Africa is the study of man's rudimentary mind; when subject to the agency of material nature, he neither progresses nor retrogrades. He would appear rather a degeneracy from the civilised man than a savage rising to the first step, were it not for his apparent incapacity for improvement. . . . He seems to belong to one of these childish races which, never rising to man's estate, fall like worn-out links from the great chain of animated nature. . . . [The African] has stopped short at the threshold of progress; he shows no signs of development; no higher and more varied orders of intellect are called into being. . . ."[16]

The third area, that of sexuality, reveals one of Burton's major abiding interests. From his early days in India, when he got himself into lasting trouble by producing a firsthand report on male homosexual brothels in Karachi, to the publication, in his later years, of translations of Indian and Arabian erotica and of his famous unexpurgated *Arabian Nights,* Burton showed a lively personal and scholarly interest in the range and variety of human sexual experience (as will be discussed more fully in a later chapter). So while in Africa he studied native sexual practices, both by observation and, as he rather slyly suggests, personal experience, and he gathered evidence of the black African's reputed sexual prowess and vitality. Apparently he found the natives receptive to his investigations, at least in some tribes. He examined, measured, compared, collected legends, and produced descriptions which he tried to offer as evidence of the African's lowly nature but from which he could not erase a marked strain of personal envy.[17] These accounts were, inevitably, deleted from the earlier editions of his books and were either privately printed or added as appendixes to later editions. In contributing to one of the most firmly established of myths, or stereotypes, of the African, Burton may not appear to everyone as being necessarily pejorative—except that such evidence, along with that of other writers, was often used to support an image of black bestiality, of closeness to the animal world.

At one point, having filled many pages with negative commentary, Burton paused to assure the reader that he is not giving a distorted picture of the African: "The ethnologist who compares this sketch with the far more favourable description of the Kafirs, a kindred race, given by travellers in South Africa, may suspect that only the darker shades of the picture are placed before the eye. But, as will appear in a future page, much of this moral degradation must be attributed to the working, through centuries, of the slave-trade; the tribes are no longer as nature made them; and from their connection with strangers they have derived nothing but corruption."[18]

Burton devotes many pages to describing the slave trade and showing its effects on African culture and character. He stresses that these areas, East and West, suffered from great poverty and were more than usually disturbed. The tribes fought and raided one another desperately and appeared to be completely demoralized, largely because of the slave trade. Burton emphasizes that those parts of Africa he had explored had been for hundreds of years subject to the corrupting influence of slavery, with the result that, seduced by the promise of relatively easy profits, the native tribes of these regions had bought into the slave business. In fact, for some tribes it appeared to be their only business—slaves both for export and for domestic use—and the consequences had been a slow and steady demoralization, a social corruption and moral apathy. Burton states that the practice of slavery, when combined with impossible climatic conditions and widespread disease, could paralyze and erode any culture.

It is curious, however, that Burton, even while recognizing, and calling attention to, some major causes of African barbarism, persisted in his claims that the black was by nature inferior, a "lesser breed" destined to eternal subordination. In expressing this view, Burton was only unusually outspoken—he was not unique. And while he was an acute observer, he was not an original thinker. He reflected the values of his time, as did most other African explorers. He did, however, try to make certain discriminations. For example, his remarks about the East African tend to be more charitable than those he makes about the West African, possibly because the natives of Somaliland were, to Burton's mind, less "negroid" and more under the influence of a "beneficent" Islamic culture than were the natives of the West coast.[19] He concludes *The Lake Regions of Central Africa* with hope of an improved life for East Africans. He assures his readers that, despite its strong hold in Africa, "the extinction of slavery would be hailed with delight by the great mass throughout the length and breadth of Eastern Africa. This people, 'robbed and spoiled' by their oppressors, who are legionary, call themselves 'the meat,' and the slave-dealers 'the knife': they hate and fear their own demon Moloch, but they lack unanimity to free their necks from his yoke. Africa still 'lies in her blood,' but the progress of human society, and the straiter bonds which unite man with man, shall eventually rescue her from her old pitiable fate."[20]

These are commendable words—"progress of human society" and "bonds which unite man with man"—and they perhaps represent Burton's more basic feelings about the African (at least the East African), as do the more balanced reports delivered to government and professional societies; but they are not strong enough, nor do they appear often enough, to offset the major image, that of the essentially subhuman status of the African Negro, which Burton's writings helped to foster.

The City of the Saints and Across the Rocky Mountains to California

In 1860, after publication of the *Lake Regions* and the tragic controversy with John Speke, Burton had had enough of Africa and decided to visit an area that had long held his interest—North America, especially the West. He gave as his reasons for making the trip his desire to add Salt Lake City to his list of holy cities and to compare the "American Mecca" with the others he had visited; to study the American Indians and enjoy "a little skirmishing with the savages"; and to check out the various potential routes for a transcontinental railroad.

The resulting book, *The City of the Saints* (1861),[21] is a cheerful account of his travels, lacking in the acerbity and harsh judgments found in most of his other travel books. It is composed of three parts: an account of a trek from St. Joseph, Missouri, begun on 7 August 1860, across the Western prairies and into the Rocky mountains; a description and discussion of Salt Lake City and the Mormons; and an account of the trip from Salt Lake City to the Pacific.

Description of the journey: the American Indians. The first part begins in typical Burton fashion: the sense of excitement and adventure accompanying the elaborate preparations for a long and hazardous expedition. He describes these preparations in detail: the required equipment—or the "kit" and "toilet," as Burton expresses it—with comments regarding clothing, weapons, medications, maps, and other accessories. He even includes precise instructions for using and caring for the various guns to be taken along, and an explanation of the superiority of mules over horses for such an expedition—a compendium of useful information for travelers who might follow after him.

The journey is narrated with the usual close observation of the terrain, conditions of travel, weather, local fauna and flora, missionaries encountered along the way, and, above all, Indians. Just as in his earlier works, Burton is fascinated by the native peoples and portrays them in detail, his descriptions being supplemented by his own drawings. He makes generalizations about and distinctions between the tribes and their cultures and provides his usual strong opinions about the significance and quality of their various life-styles. His narrative suggests that he knows far more about the Indian cultures than his brief personal experiences could have taught him; it is apparent that he draws upon other books and traveler's reports to supplement his own observations.

One distinctive, and doubtless inevitable, feature of his narrative is that he continually draws comparisons between the American Indians and the peoples he encountered in the Near East and Africa—their appearance, customs, vices and virtues, and practices in love and war.[22] There is a long section on scalping, in which he points out that it is a universal practice—he had first discovered it in the Middle East and India. And as a serious student of language, he learned and reported what he could about the native speech and elaborate systems of pantomime. He includes a "glossary" of Indian sign-language—for example: "Peace—Intertwine the fingers of both hands" and "Today—Touch the nose with the index tip, and motion with the fist toward the ground" (128–29). He was equally fascinated by local white American speech and pronunciation, giving as examples such terms as "crik" for creek, "skeery" for scary, "drink" for a body of water, "neck of the woods," and other colorful Americanisms. And, of course, when speaking of the Indians, he gave his usual attention to the native sexual and marital rites.

Burton saw and described the American Indians very definitely as savages, but not as the depraved monsters he thought them to be before he actually encountered them. He portrays them, if not sympathetically at least impartially—except in one matter that always evoked his sarcasm. His comments on their capacity for becoming "christianised" are very similar to those he had made earlier about converts he had met in Goa: "I do not believe that an Indian of the plains ever became a Christian. He must first be humanised, then civilised, and lastly christianised; and, as has been said before, I doubt his surviving the operation" (115).

When not offering such personal opinions, Burton gathered and reported some highly interesting folklore—and it is in this area that Burton's book is especially rewarding to the modern reader. For example, his comments on Indian attitudes toward personal names and the process of naming: "The white stranger is ever offending Indian etiquette by asking the savage 'What's your name?' The person looks aside for a friend to assist him; he has learned in boyhood that some misfortune will happen to him if he discloses his name. Even husbands and wives never mention each others' names. The same practice prevails in many parts of Asia" (116).

Salt Lake City and the Mormons.   Burton devotes a considerable portion of his book to his few weeks in Salt Lake City. He thoroughly enjoyed his visit there and writes of it with enthusiasm.

He was welcomed into homes and was able to observe firsthand that aspect of the Mormon society that most interested him—the polygamic marriage. For the most part he wrote approvingly of what he saw and came to understand that controversial institution: "The Mormon household has been described by its enemies as a hell of envy, hatred, and malice, a den of murder and suicide. The same has been said of the Moslem harem. Both, I believe, suffer from the assertions of prejudice or ignorance. The temper of the new is so far superior to that of the old country, that, incredible as the statement may appear, rival wives do dwell together in amity; and do quote the proverb 'the more the merrier'. . . . I believe that many a 'happy English home' is far stormier despite the presence of monogamy' (254). He also points out that Mormon polygamy was essentially puritanical, with extreme penalties for adultery. But he was also very aware of what was wrong with polygamic marriage: "The choice egotism of the heart called Love . . . subsides into a calm and unimpassioned domestic attachment: romance and reverence are transferred, with the true Mormon concentration, from Love and Liberty to Religion and the Church. The consent of the first wife to a rival is seldom refused, and a *menage à trois,* in the Mormon sense of the phrase, is fatal to the development of that tender tie which must be confined to two. In its stead there is household comfort, affection, circumspect friendship, and domestic discipline." He adds that the result, in his view, is a subtle and pervasive atmosphere of gloom.[23] These are very interesting and perceptive words, coming from a man for whom, in his own married life, the "tender tie which must be confined to two," did not seem to loom very large.

Burton's literary technique.   In many ways *The City of the Saints* represents the writer Burton at his best—at least in the sense that he is throughout good-humored and fair-minded, and he writes with verve and clarity, without his usual addiction to obscure terminology and esoteric allusions. He does indulge, however, his addiction to detail, a compulsion that he defends in his preface. Here he is justifying not only the present book but all of his previous travel books. He begins his defense of details by quoting Boswell's comment in the latter's *Journey to the Western Islands* to the effect that while "these diminutive observations seem to take away something from the dignity of writing," they also add something. Burton cites Boswell's reminder that "life consists not of a series of illustrious

actions or elegant enjoyments." The greater part of our time "passes
in compliance with necessities, in the performance of daily duties,
in the removal of small inconveniences, in the procurement of petty
pleasures. . . ." Burton wholeheartedly agrees that the writer should
"copy Nature," not confining himself "to the great, the good, and
the beautiful" (which he translates as "the claims of cotton, civilization, and Christianity") (ix).

He cites Boswell further: "There is yet another cause of error not
always easily surmounted, though more dangerous to the veracity
of intinerary narratives than imperfect mensuration." And that is
the deferring of description to a later and more convenient time:
"How much a few hours take from certainty of knowledge and
distinctness of imagery . . . how rapidly separate parts will be
confused . . . particular features and discriminations will be found
compressed [into] one gross and general idea" (ix–x). These words
are "worthy to be written in 'letters of gold,' " says Burton, who
then proceeds to narrate his story fortified in the methods that he
had always believed in and used in his travel books.

Chapter Six
Burton as Translator and Poet

During the years he spent in South America, Burton wrote, as he always did, some books on the regions he visited—*The Highlands of Brazil* (1869) and *Letters from the Battle-fields of Paraguay* (1870). These works are informative, scholarly, and detailed, and contain most of the same virtues and faults of his earlier books of travel. He also translated and annotated *The Lands of Cazembe, Lacerda's Journey to Cazembe in 1798* (1873), and he annotated Albert Tootal's translation of *The Captivity of Hans Stade of Hesse, in A.D. 1547–1555, Among the Wild Tribes of Eastern Brazil* (1874). But of principal importance and interest from a literary standpoint are Burton's own poetic efforts and his translations of the literatures of Portugal and the Middle East during the 1870s and 1880s.

During the 1870s Burton was known to the reading public primarily as an explorer and author of notable books of travel, but he also had another, well-concealed side to his nature: he considered himself to be a man of letters, a poet, and a translator. For regardless of what other projects commanded his immediate attention, Burton, since his earliest days in India, assiduously collected manuscripts and other materials containing the imaginative literature of the region where he happened to be stationed, and he usually worked on several literary projects at the same time. While in India, he not only took notes and wrote his books of Indian travel, he also translated the "Pilpay's Fables," which were never published; he read and collected materials in modern Indian languages as well as Sanskrit, and read whatever original versions of the *Arabian Nights* he could get his hands on. Most of his Indian manuscripts were destroyed in a warehouse fire in London shortly after his marriage, but he salvaged what he could and took steps to replace the missing materials whenever possible. These collections enabled him, while stationed in Brazil, to divide his time between several projects: a grammar of the Tupy-Guarani language, which was never published;

his monumental translation of the Portuguese poet Camoens's *The Lusiads;* his translation, or "adaptation," as he called it, of a volume of Hindu folktales; his anonymously produced philosophical poem, *The Kasidah of Haji Abdu El-Yezdi;* and his translation of *The Arabian Nights.*

Vikram and the Vampire

In this work, Burton chose to concentrate, out of a considerable body of Hindu writings, on the *Vetala-pancha-Vinshati,* or *Twenty-five Tales of a Demon.* These were a part of a large collection of folk literature written originally in Sanskrit and dating back to the eleventh century. Working with a 1799 Hindi version, Burton "adapted" eleven of the twenty-five tales, which were published as *Vikram and the Vampire, or Tales of Hindu Devilry* (1870).[1] Apparently he was the first to make available to English readers these ancient ironic tales of fantasy and magic. His efforts, however, were not appreciated, as the volume sold poorly and lost money—perhaps because the tales do not live up to the promise of the intriguing title. Isabel Burton, in her preface to the volume, raises the reader's expectations: "The Baital-Pachisi, or Twenty-five Tales of a Baital, is the history of a huge Bat, Vampire, or Evil Spirit which inhabited and animated dead bodies." And a recent scholar observes: "It is curious that out of all the Hindu and Arabic literature [Burton] could have translated, he chose first that particular sequence of stories in which the story-teller—normally a vagrant hero like himself—is here pictured as a monster feeding on corpses and sucking the blood of the living."[2] The monster does indeed tell the stories, but he appears only in the introductory section and the tales he tells are relatively mild and lacking in "devilry."

The introductory section (which does contain some scenes of the hideous and monstrous) presents a historical account of a great king named Raja Vikram, the "King Arthur of the East." In one of his last adventures he encounters a Jogi, or magician, in a nightmarish nocturnal scene that takes place at a burning-ground for corpses populated by "hideous bestial forms" and the ghostly shapes of the dead waiting for new bodies to inhabit: "The spirits of those that had been foully slain wandered about with gashed limbs; and skeletons, whose mouldy bones were held together by bits of blackened sinew, followed them as the murderer does his victim. Malignant witches with shrivelled skins, horrid eyes and distorted forms, crawled and crouched over the earth; whilst spectres and goblins now stood motionless, and tall as lofty palm trees; then as if in fits, leaped, danced, and tumbled before their evocator. The air was filled with shrill and strident cries . . ." (32).

Vikram promises the Jogi that he would venture into forbidding regions and bring back the Baital, or Vampire. So Vikram, along with his son, leaves the Jogi's ghoulish realm to seek the evil creature, who is soon found hanging, as is its custom, head down from a tree branch. Its body, brown like "an over-dried coconut," was "thin and ribbed like a skeleton or a bamboo framework, and as it held on to a bough, like a flying-fox [a large bat] by the toe-tips, its drawn muscles stood out as if they were ropes of coir. Blood it appeared to have none . . . and as the Raja handled its skin, it felt icy cold and clammy as might a snake. The only sign of life was the whisking of a ragged little tail much resembling a goat's" (35–36).

This grotesque creature turns out to be less than dangerous, however. In fact, the ensuing scenes are a series of comic efforts on the part of Vikram and his son to get the Baital into a sack—and to keep him there, as he proves to be an agile escape-artist. But when finally bagged (he will make several temporary escapes during the ensuing journey) he turns out to be quite sociable and talkative, and the remainder of the book consists of the tales he recounts while bouncing along in his sack on Vikram's back.

The tales, in the manner of good fables, all have points to make which are suggested in their titles: "In which a Man deceived a Woman," "Of the relative Villainy of Men and Women," "Of a Woman who Told the Truth," "Showing the exceeding Folly of many Wise Fools," and one of the best of the tales, "Showing that a Man's Wife belongs not to his Body but to his Head." The stories have nothing to do with vampires and little with devilry. They are pre–Arabian Nights fables involving traditional plots such as, for example, three suitors for the hand of a beautiful princess and their diverse attempts to win the prize. As in fairy tales there are giants and sorcerers, wise old women and magic spells, virtuous youths and their evil brothers, and such. An interesting aspect of some of the stories is their presenting the listener with a problem—he is often left to decide who is right: which suitor should win the princess, or, should a young bride feel greatest loyalty to a strange body which is wearing her husband's head, or to a strange head on her husband's body?

Another point of interest is the persistent antifeminine bias, which will appear in full bloom later in Burton's translation of *The Arabian Nights*. The text abounds in such comments as: "but she concealed this motive in the depths of her thought, enlarging, as women are apt to do, upon everything but the truth" (14); "The pretty queen, placing both hands upon her husband's bosom, kissed his eyes and his lips, and sweetly smiling on his face—for great is the guile of women, whispered . . ." (15); "For there can be nothing thoroughly bad unless a woman is at the bottom of it . . ." (25); and so on.

But it should be stated that these remarks, which appear sexist by modern standards, are matched by equally satirical observations on the greed, lust, cowardice, and folly of men, and apparently Burton's wife found nothing in these stories to offend her feminine sensibilities. She thought the book to be delightfully entertaining, but apparently the reading public did not share her enthusiasm. The work attracted little critical attention and few readers, and it remained largely unnoticed until its reprinting in 1969.

The Kasidah of Haji Abdu El-Yezdi

When Burton published *The Kasidah of Haji Abdu El-Yezdi* (1880),[3] a long poem, he decided, as he did with many of his later erotic works and with an earlier poem called *Stone Talk,* to use a pseudonym. He presented the *Kasidah* as the work of an old Persian friend who had allegedly given him the manuscript for translation. But Burton concealed even his identity as translator and editor, attributing the role to "F. B." (Frank from his middle name, and Baker from his mother's maiden name). He added to the deception of the "Oriental poem" by having F. B. analyze the work in critical notes and add footnotes that explained certain Oriental metaphors. He never publicly admitted to being the author.

Burton began the poem in the 1850s and worked on it until its publication in 1880. As it shows a preoccupation with mental decline and physical decay associated with aging, it was doubtless written largely during his later years:

> Hardly we learn to wield the blade
> before the wrist grows stiff and old;

> Hardly we learn to ply the pen
> ere Thought and Fancy faint with cold.

The notes at the end of the poem (which equal the length of the poem itself) begin with a brief biography of the "author," Haji Abdu El-Yezdi, who of course strongly resembles Burton. Burton, as F. B., doubtless enjoyed slipping in such sly remarks as "Haji Abdu has been known to me for more years than I care to record" and "Even his intimates were ignorant of the fact that he had a skeleton in his cupboard, his Kasidah or distichs [poetic couplets]"—all were unaware that he "woo'd the Muse" (71–72). He tells how the manuscript was given to him somewhere "in Western India," then gives a summary and explanation of the contents of the poem—the poet's efforts to find and express a religious, metaphysical, and moral system of his own. F. B. also lays out the poem's principal "message" in his "To the Reader":

The Translator has ventured to entitle a "Lay of the Higher Law" the following composition, which aims at being in advance of its time; and he has not reared the danger of collision with such unpleasant forms as the "Higher Culture." The principles which justify the name are as follows:—

The Author asserts that Happiness and Misery are equally divided and distributed in the world.

He makes Self-cultivation, with due regard to others, the sole and sufficient object of human life.

He suggests that the affections, the sympathies, and the "divine gift of Pity" are man's highest enjoyments.

He advocates suspension of judgments, with a proper suspicion of "Facts, the idlest of superstitions."

Finally, although destructive to appearance, he is essentially reconstructive.

For other details concerning the Poem and the Poet, the curious reader is referred to the end of the volume.

Before setting forth the Haji's philosophy, F. B. discusses the shortcomings of all previous and existing systems of belief. He states that the Haji's views can best be described as fatalism tempered by skepticism: with the Haji Abdu "suspension of judgment is a system" (79). F. B. claims that the *Kasidah* (which translates as "tes-

tament") is pessimistic but not nihilistic: its "healthy wail" is "over
the shortness and miseries of life."

F. B. lists the various miseries of human existence, but exempts
the Deity from responsibility: "the theory of a beneficent or mal-
eficent deity is a purely sentimental fancy, contradicted by human
reason and the aspect of the world" (83). But he denies that Haji
Abdu is intentionally irreverent—his mind is Oriental, with com-
plexities and seeming paradoxes that baffle the Westerner, for the
Haji is one who "believes in everything equally and generally may
be said to believe in nothing." His views, as "modified fatalism,"
are also highly individualistic. F. B. quotes from the poem: "Never
repent because thy will with will of Fate be not at one; / Think,
thou please, before thou dost, but never rue the deed when done"
(87). One must accept responsibility for one's own actions and
beliefs, and reject "all popular and mythological explanations by
the Fall of 'Adam,' the innate depravity of human nature, and the
absolute perfection of certain Incarnations, which argues their di-
vinity. He can only wail over the prevalence of evil, assume its
foundation to be error, and purpose to abate it by uprooting that
Ignorance which bears and feeds it" (95). The Haji believed that
the soul was only "a convenient word denoting the sense of personality, of individual identity." Conscience, he asserts, is only a
matter of geographical and temporal accident, and Christian and
Moslem ideas of heaven are merely idealized copies of the earthly
present.

The poem begins with a description of dawn over the desert:

> The hour is nigh; the waning Queen
>   walks forth to rule the later night;
> Crown'd with the sparkle of a Star,
>   and throned on orb of ashen light:
> The Wolf-tail [the false dawn] sweeps the paling East
>   to leave a deeper gloom behind,
> And Dawn uprears her shining head,
>   sighing with semblance to a wind.

He then goes on to lament the speed with which life quickens as
it nears its end:

> Mine eyes, my brains, my heart, are sad,—
>   sad is the very core of me:

> All wearies, changes, passes, ends;
>   alas, the Birthday's injury!

(12)

and later:

> Yes, Life in youth-tide standeth still;
>   in manhood streameth soft and slow;
> See, as it nears the abysmal goal,
>   how fleet the waters flash and flow!

(23)

After these lamentations the poet shifts to his philosophy which rejects all conventional notions of afterlife, including those of Moslem and Christian faith, especially Christianity,

> Whose saddening creed of herited Sin
>   spilt o'er the world its cold gray spell;
> In every vista showed a grave,
>   and 'neath the grave the glare of Hell;
> Till all Life's Poesy sinks to prose;
>   romance to dull Reality fades;
> Earth's flush of gladness pales in gloom
>   and God again to man degrades.

(33)

And he says of man's various faiths:

> All Faith is false, all Faith is true:
>   Truth is the shattered mirror strown
> In myriad bits; while each believes
>   this little bit the whole to own.

(41)

The poem expresses the Haji's (Burton's) beliefs on a variety of subjects, and invariably gives a subjectivist point of view—the individual man is the center of the universe, the creator of his own meanings and values:

> There is no Good, there is no Bad;
>   these be the whims of mortal will;

> What works me weal that I call "good"
>   What harms and hurts I hold as "ill."
>   (35)

Burton's views on evolution, which were implied in comments in his earlier books involving the "unevolved" black race, are here reiterated:

> The race of Being from dawn of Life
>   in an unbroken course was run;
> What men are pleased to call their Souls
>   was in the hog and dog begun.
>   (46)

What a man should believe and how he discovers the truth are found in one of his best known quatrains:

> Do what thy manhood bids thee do,
>   from none but self expect applause;
> He noblest lives and noblest dies
>   who makes and keeps his self-made laws.
>   (57)

He concludes the poem with traditional Arab symbols of life and death: the desert wind and the coming of the camel (as distinct from the Bible's "pale horse") with the tinkling bell:

> In Days to come, Days slow to dawn
>   when Wisdom deigns to dwell with men,
> These echoes of a voice song stilled
>   haply shall wake responsive strain:
> Wend now thy way with brow serene,
>   fear not thy humble tale to tell:—
> The whispers of the Desert-wind;
>   the tinkling of the camel's bell.
>   (66–67)

The *Kasidah* was privately printed, and the first reviews appeared twenty years later. Of the first edition less than a hundred copies were sold. Yet it became one of Burton's most popular books. While not attaining to the widespread popularity of Edward Fitzgerald's

The Rubaiyat of Omar Khayyam, which had been published some years earlier and which Burton was doubtless aware of while working on his own poem, the *Kasidah* has been frequently reprinted. Burton would doubtless have been pleased that his anonymous poetic efforts, which contained his candid statements of belief (or nonbelief), were so well received. As a publisher of the 1965 reprint said in a publisher's note—with a completely straight face: "Long out of print, this book is published again in the belief that its message is of significance for our times. *The Kasidah* is the spiritual message of Haji Abdu, known through Islam as *Nabbiana,* 'Our Prophet.' It presents the contradictions, the mysteries, the meaning of all existence, and seeks to answer the old, old question, what is truth. The many readers who have found inspiration and solace in the writings of Kahlil Gibran will find the same in *The Kasidah.*"

The Arabian Nights

During the 1880s, while stationed in Trieste, Burton's health grew steadily worse. He had to admit that his traveling days were over, and he accordingly threw what energies remained to him—and they were considerable—into the one activity still open to him: writing. In 1884 he began to rework and organize for publication his translation of the *Book of a Thousand Nights and a Night (Alf Laila Wa Laila,* sometimes spelled *Alf Layla Wa Layla),* popularly known as *The Arabian Nights.*[4] He had first begun work on *The Arabian Nights* some thirty-two years earlier in India. There had also been time, while living in Aden, to have long talks with his friend and fellow orientalist John Steinhaeuser, about his collection of Arabic folklore. Some of the tales, thoroughly expurgated, were well known in England and were considered suitable reading for children. But both Burton and Steinhaeuser had read and heard the stories in the original and knew full well what they were about. "The most familiar book in England next to the Bible," Burton wrote, "it is the least known, the reason being that about one-fifth is utterly unfit for translation, and the most sanguine Orientalist would not dare render more than three-quarters of the remainder." Despite these reservations, Burton and his friend seriously considered the idea of making a "full, complete, unvarnished, uncastrated, copy of the great original," with Burton translating the poetry and Steinhaeuser the prose.[5]

They corresponded on the project for many years, but when Stein-haeuser died his papers were lost. Burton therefore decided to con-tinue the translation on his own. He worked off and on until 1881, when he discovered that a fellow scholar, John Payne (1842–1916), had also been doing a translation of *The Arabian Nights* which was about to be published. Burton, however, saw no reason why he should not go ahead with his own. He wrote to Payne, offering his help in any way that Payne should wish, and they developed a friendly relationship. Burton also discovered that Payne's edition was limited to 500 copies and was not fully annotated, whereas he, Burton, wanted to make his version "a book whose speciality is Anthropology." So he persevered.[6]

There existed no complete written source for *The Arabian Nights,* which are a collection of anonymous folktales, so Burton, in com-piling his version, used no less than twenty-one other translations and manuscripts to make up his original ten-volume work, and still more manuscripts to produce his six-volume supplement. In order to be sure that a work of such a nature would find a publisher, Burton made special arrangements. As the title page of the original edition says, it was "Printed by the Kamashastra Society for Private Subscribers only." The purpose of the society was to publish trans-lations of Oriental literature of an erotic nature, and it existed only from 1883 until Burton's death in 1890. During this period the society brought out five titles of erotica (to be discussed in a sub-sequent chapter) and in 1885 produced the first volume of *The Arabian Nights,* bearing the title of *A Plain and Literal Translation of the Arabian Night's Entertainments, Now Entitled The Book of the Thousand Nights and a Night.* It was dedicated to John Frederick Steinhaeuser.

It seems inevitable that Burton would translate and annotate *The Arabian Nights.* His entire life, in a sense, was a preparation for this vast undertaking, and working with *The Arabian Nights* provided him the opportunity to draw on his enormous storehouse of knowl-edge about the East, to utilize his collection of anthropological lore as well as to display his ideas, opinions, and prejudices which for the most part had not changed since his early years in the Middle East and Africa. He could also work with his favorite Eastern lan-guage, Arabic, and his preferred culture. He had early expressed his admiration for the Persians, and was familiar with the details of Persian life on all levels of society.

The World of *The Arabian Nights*

The tales center in and around the fabled city of Baghdad under the reign of the great khalif, Haroun er Rashid (or Harun al-Rashid), during the early ninth century, a reign usually chosen by Muslim historians as representing the khalifate in its golden age. At that time, Baghdad, situated on the banks of the Tigris River in Persia, was a city of beauty and pleasure, as the tales make clear. It has been described as the jewel of Persian culture, surrounded by gardens and groves of orange, lime, tamarisk, and myrtle, luxuriating in a plenitude of precious water—natural and artificial streams, fountains, and pools, living waters whose charms were often enhanced by perfumes and rose-water. The city was celebrated by many a Persian poet, who considered it a terrestial paradise, a preview of the celestial—a city of flowers and music: the songs of birds, the lilting strains of lutes, the melodies of the "houris" emanating from the gardens and palace courtyards. Evenings were scenes of moonlight, mystery, and romance, with musk and other exotic perfumes hanging heavy in the air—the perfect setting for the narrator of *The Arabian Nights,* the ingenious Sharazad,[7] to spin her tales of love, lust, greed, bravery, and treachery.[8]

The whole world of medieval Persia is brought to life in these vivid pages, and Burton reveled in his ability to render them into vigorous English prose and poetry. He was especially delighted, and liberated, by the refreshing Eastern candor: in these tales nothing is rejected as improper, unwholesome, or unclear. Every type and class of society is represented—king and slave, nobles and peasants, priests and sorcerers, the faithful and the treacherous, the wise and the foolish, the pious and the debauched. And every type of story is here: histories of actual events, supernatural tales and romances, anecdotes and short stories dealing with everyday life, fictitious tales of actual historical personages, accounts of rogues, con men, imposters, assassins, and rascals of all sorts (who will reappear in European "picaresque tales"). The most numerous tales are those involving the fantastic, including accounts of saints and miracles, unfortunate lovers, fables of moral intent, and bawdy tales (which will influence the later Boccaccio).[9]

The Arabian Nights tales, in their frequent emphasis on sexuality and the nature of women, might seem to be made to order for a Burton to express certain of his obsessions and biases. He seems to revel in the sexual attitudes displayed in many of the tales—indeed, the major cause for the tales being told is the deceitfulness and sexual lust of women, and Burton recounts them with relish and gusto. The "frame-tale," which encompasses the various stories and provides the rationale for the storytelling, depicts the King Shahryar and his brother discovering, quite by accident, that their beautiful young wives were in the habit of engaging in lustful orgies with the slaves whenever the two kings were out of town. Once discovered, the wives and lovers are summarily slain, and the two brothers set out on a quest to ascertain if all women are so deceitful. They find out that it is indeed true—in an episode in which a "captive wife" forces the two brothers to have sexual relations with her while her captor-husband, a giant Jenni (genie), is asleep. She brags of her many sexual conquests while duping her stupid husband.

King Shahryar, thoroughly disillusioned—"there never was nor is there one chaste woman upon the face of earth"—decides on the only way to insure the fidelity of his wives: to marry a proven virgin, sleep with her one night, and kill her the next morning. The supply of available virgins begins to run low until Sharazad, in an attempt to end the slaughter and to save the reputation of her father, the vizier, who was responsible for supplying the new wives, offers herself as the next in line. Being an exceptionally clever and erudite young woman, she succeeds in postponing her own morning execution by telling fascinating tales every night which were unfinished by daybreak, causing the king to eagerly await the continuation the next night. After 1,001 such nights, and three children born to him, King Shahryar abandons his original plan, admits that he has a truly wonderful and faithful wife, and *The Arabian Nights* are concluded with a joyous formal wedding affirming the permanence of their union. Thus while many of the tales are slanderous of women, the overall structure of the tales reveals an intelligent and talented woman leading a misguided king out of his murderous convictions, into a balanced view of woman as a human being, and back into the esteem of his people, who had been very upset by their king's practices.[10]

Burton, however, takes full advantage of the beginning of the frame-tale to portray, in colorful detail supported by footnotes, the "debauched woman." The opening pages provide a clear insight into Burton's style and the way in which his attitudes and biases, especially his strong racial prejudice, influence his choice of words.

In the incident of the wives' infidelity—their carrying on orgies with the slaves—the chosen lovers happen to be Negro; and as seen in his earlier work on Africa, Burton was convinced of the black man's superior sexual prowess which so attracted the "lustful woman." Here it is interesting and revealing to compare translations. The following is Payne's translation which Burton had before him when making his own: "Out came twenty damsels and twenty black slaves, and among them his brother's wife, who was wonderfully fair and beautiful. They all came up to a fountain, where the girls and slaves took off their clothes and sat down together. Then the queen called out, 'O Mesoud!' And there came to her a black slave, who embraced her and she him. Then he lay with her, and on like wise did the other slaves with the girls. And they ceased not from kissing and clipping and clicketing and carousing until the day began to wane."[11] Burton's translation is much like Payne's until the queen summons her black lover: "And then sprang with a drop-leap from one of the trees a big slobbering blackamoor with rolling eyes which showed the whites, a truly hideous sight. He walked boldly up to her and threw his arms around her neck while she embraced him as warmly; then he bussed her and enjoyed her. On like wise did the other slaves with the girls till all had satisfied their passions" (1:6). Payne translates an earlier passage, in which the king, who had departed on a journey, returns unexpectedly to his palace, as: he "entered his apartments, where he found his wife asleep in his own bed, in the arms of one of his black slaves." Burton renders this scene as follows: "he entered his apartments, where he found the Queen, his wife, asleep on his own carpet-bed, embracing with both arms a black cook of loathsome aspect and foul with kitchen grease and grime." A later rerun of this scene, in which the king invites his brother to see for himself, again features the "hideous blackamoor." "The lady laughed heartily, and all fell to satisfying their lusts, and remained so occupied for a couple of hours" until "the blackamoor dismounted from the Queen's bosom" (1:9).

In a footnote Burton provides what he is sure is the cause of the queen's activities, in which she must have known she was risking discovery and certain death: "debauched women preferred negroes on account of the size of their parts. . . . In my time no honest Hindi Moslem would take his women-folk to Zanzibar on account of the huge attractions and enormous temptations there and thereby offered to them" (1:6).

In order to heighten the horror which his Victorian readers were presumably supposed to experience on reading of these sexual encounters, Burton not only describes the Negro lovers as hideous, filthy, and loathsome, but also portrays the woman as fair, lovely, winsome, and ladylike. The king's wife is "wondrous fair, a model of beauty and comeliness and symmetry and perfect loveliness and who paced with the grace of a gazelle." The wife of the cuckolded Jenni, who claims to have enjoyed hundreds of men, is described as "white-skinned and of winsomest mien, of stature fine and thin." Thus the point is made: beneath the surface loveliness and ladylike delicacy lies a seething mass of lusts. It is this tendency to dramatize, even emphasize, sexual debauchery that distinguishes Burton's work from those of other Victorian translators.

But even Burton was put off by some of the tales. Sometimes he stands back from his own translations and comments on them. Regarding the "Story of the Three Witches" (in volume 6), he says, "It is the grossest and most brutal satire on the sex, suggesting that a woman would prefer an additional inch of penis to anything this world or the next can offer her." He even commends some stories for their admirable delicacy; but whenever a character named Abu Nowes appears, Burton issues a warning: "All but anthropological students are advised to 'skip' over anecdotes in which his name and abominations occur." Abu Nowes, it seems, "loved to sport and make merry with fair boys and cull the rose from every brightly blooming cheek" (5:67–69).

Some stories contain passages so revolting that even Burton was repelled by them. "Nauseous" is his word for one tale in which a woman bakes bread from dough that had been used as a dressing for a "corroding ulcer" on a man's spine. But, on the other hand, *The Arabian Nights* contain many tales and passages of great charm, such as the following, which Burton has rendered into rich and full-flavored English:

The girl is soft of speech, fair of form like a branchlet of basil, with teeth like chamomile-petals and hair like halters wherefrom to hand hearts. Her cheeks are like blood-red anemones and her face like a pippin: she has lips like wine and breasts like pomegranates twain and a shape supple as a rattan-cane. . . . And she hath a bosom, as it were a way between two hills which are a pair of breasts like globes of ivory sheen; likewise, a stomach right smooth, flanks soft as the palm-spathe and creased with folds and dimples which overlap one another, and liberal thighs, which like columns of pearl arise, and back parts which billow and beat together like seas of glass or mountains of glance, and two feet and hands of gracious mould like unto ingots of virgin gold. (3:226)

The Translations: Criticism and Controversy

But Burton also has another style of translation, one not as engaging as this poetic echo of the King James Bible. In his attempt to write "as an Arab would have written in English" and to capture the "Oriental quaintness" of the medieval Arab, Burton's version includes a myriad of bizarre and original words. As he did in all his translations, he drew heavily on archaic English, on foreign words, or, if those did not suffice, on words of his own creation— sometimes awkward terms like "grievousest" and "grievouser" or medieval words like "ensorceled." He was Victorian enough to avoid most Anglo-Saxon four-letter words but would use their equivalents from other sources, like the Norse "skite" and "coynte." And always he preferred the old-fashioned diction: "thou" and "thee," "hath" and "goest," which seemed to him appropriate to the time period of *The Arabian Nights* but which did not blend well with such modern expressions as "a red cent," "belle and Belledame," "a veritable beauty of a man," "O, my cuss," "thy hubby," "a Charley."

One scholar, who pointed out some of these "perversities of style," claims that they make Burton's translation "unreadable." Such terms "may possibly have Arabic equivalents but certainly cannot render them for us. No illusion can survive such barbarisms." Burton's work may be "truly great," but to the English reader "it gives no true idea of the original, and nothing could be further from being an English classic. No one will ever delight in it; many will study it."[12] Burton seemed to have anticipated such criticism: "I have never hesitated to coin a word when wanted, such as 'she snorted and snarked,' fully to represent the original. These, like many in Rabelais, are mere barbarisms unless generally accepted; in which case they become civilised and common currency" (1:xiv).

The publication of Burton's *Arabian Nights* in 1885 precipitated a lively ongoing controversy about the quality and originality of his translations. Some scholars may have questioned his scholarship but essentially it was his "Englishing" that roused the critics—on both sides of the argument. The "Burton-Payne Controversy" centered on the question of plagiarism—the extent to which Burton had, or had not, lifted words and passages from Payne. There were, to be sure, translations other than Payne's in existence, and Burton used them all. One able precurser was Henry Torrens, an Irish novelist and poet, who brought out a partial version in 1830 and died before completing his work. Another well qualified translator was Edward William Lane. He had a thorough knowledge of Arabian life and language, but his versions, which appeared between 1839 and 1841, were incomplete. He avoided the "objectionable" tales and produced a book, according to Burton, intended for "the drawing-room table," not for serious scholars. Both of these writers had their backers, but Payne's version, published between 1882 and 1884, was usually seen as Burton's only real competition.[13]

Burton freely admitted his indebtedness to all his precursers. He frequently says "I have borrowed from Payne," "I give Torrens by way of specimen," "I quote from Lane," but he also criticizes other translators, more often expressing scorn than praise. He could also take an objective view of his own work: "I have carefully Englished [by which Burton means "translated"] the picturesque terms and novel expressions in all their outlandishness," and "the original is intensely prosaic—and so am I."

But these small confessions did not satisfy some critics, especially the partisans of Payne. Thomas Wright, Payne's friend and ardent admirer, wrote a biography of Burton in 1906 that was fundamentally hostile, and then, in 1919, a worshipful biography of Payne. Wright says of the book on Burton: "One of my principal objects in writing the book had been to show that Burton had stolen the translation from Payne."[14] Norman Penzer, in compiling his annotated bibliography of Burton's works, sets about to correct "Wright's absurdities,"[15] whereas Joseph Campbell, echoing Wright, flatly asserts that Burton plagiarized from Payne's version, following it "word for word, even semicolon for semicolon, not merely 'often,' but throughout."[16] Other scholars, such as J. T. Winterich, J. Oestrup, Duncan Macdonald, and Fawn Brodie, line up on different sides of the argument, usually making their points by juxtaposing passages from the two translators. Brodie, for example, demonstrates that those sections of Burton's version, when done *before* Payne's, showed a remarkable similarity.[17] Burton was always more literal than Payne, often more gross, though he tried to soften the "terrible frankness" of the tales by his archaic style, which he felt gave an "esoteric charm." It is apparent that in passages involving sexual encounters, especially homosexual, Burton was more faithful to the original text. Payne showed more "timidity." Furthermore, Burton translated more stories than Payne did. The first ten volumes included the same 1,001 stories as Payne's nine-volume version, but in his six-volume *Supplemental Nights* (1886–88) Burton included seventy-eight stories not in Payne's supplemental three volumes, *Tales from the Arabic* (1884). But on the question of the relative merits of the two translations, perhaps the last word belongs to a scholar who was himself an Arab. He asserted that both Burton and Payne failed to convey "the magic and music, the spirit-stirring lyricism of the original" and pointed out that "the Arabic rhythm, do what we may, cannot be reproduced in English."[18]

Burton's Motives and the Question of Morality

Perhaps anticipating criticism of his work, Burton claimed that his *Arabian Nights* were not intended for the public at large but for students of Orientalism and anthropologists, and that his translation, along with the detailed notes and the "Terminal Essay," were to be the definitive version for the English scholar. He states in his foreword that his aim was to provide informative addenda to the main text in order that the English-reading student could grasp the full significance of each action and statement in the tales. He wanted to furnish a sort of running commentary that would enable the student "to read between the lines" and to understand hints and innuendoes that would otherwise have been passed by unheeded (10:300). Burton was probably successful in this aim but in so doing he provoked the condemnation of those readers who felt that the heavy annotation spoiled the literary quality, the "illusion," that is required for the full enjoyment of the literature.[19] But as it turned out, Burton had it both ways: his work has been admired by the scholars while being the most widely reproduced version for the general reading public.

Burton had another reason for translating *The Arabian Nights,* one which motivated most of his other writings on the East, and that was to educate the English Foreign Office. In his earlier books he had continually complained of the ignorance of the officials sent to govern in the Middle East, and he remarks sourly in the foreword to *The Arabian Nights* that "apparently England is ever forgetting that she is at present the greatest Mohammedan empire in the world." Yet the study of "Arabism," as he called it, let alone any study of Moslem life, had been completely neglected in official examinations for the Indian Civil Service. Whenever England is called upon to handle governmental problems in Moslem lands, "she fails after a fashion which scandalises her few (very few) friends; and her crass ignorance concerning the Oriental peoples which should most interest her, exposes her to the contempt of Europe as well as of the Eastern world" (1:xxiii). His *Arabian Nights,* he hoped, would help to correct this abysmal failing in the Empire's foreign policy[20]— if, that is, the work were to attract a large and respectful audience.

In his translator's foreword Burton speaks of the "stumbling blocks" in the path of general acceptance of his *Arabian Nights:* "The simple, naive and child-like indecency which, from Tangiers to Japan, occurs throughout general conversation of high and low in the present day. The work treats in an unconventionally free and naked manner of subjects and matters which are usually, by common consent, left undescribed." He quotes the eminent Orientalist of an earlier generation, Sir William Jones: "that anything natural can be offensively obscene never seems to have occurred to the Indians or to their legislators." Burton concurs: "grossness and indecency . . . are matters of time and place. . . . I have carefully sought out the English equivalent of every Arabic word, however low it may be or 'shocking' to ears polite; preserving, on the other hand, all possible delicacy where the indecency is not intentional" (1:xv–xvi): "The general tone of *The Nights* is exceptionally high and pure. . . . Subtle corruption and covert licentiousness are utterly absent; we find more real 'vice' in many a short French *roman* . . . and in not a few English novels of our day than in the thousands of pages of the Arab. Here we have nothing of that most immodest modern modesty which sees covert implication where nothing is implied, and 'improper' allusion when propriety is not outraged." These, Burton asserts, stand in sharp contrast with the straightforward crudities of *The Arabian Nights* whose "morale is sound and healthy" (1:xvi–xvii).

However, it was not necessarily the tales themselves that outraged many critics (and attracted readers). Perhaps the most notorious part of Burton's translation was the "Terminal Essay," much of which dealt with matters the average Englishman was not accustomed to reading about.

Burton's "Terminal Essay"

The 199-page "Terminal Essay" appears at the end of volume 10, the last of the first series of the *Nights,* and it treats a variety of topics, some of which are innocuous enough: the origins of the stories, the other translations that had been made in Europe, the "matter and manner" of *The Arabian Nights,* and a commentary on rhymed prose and poetry. But the primary source of the essay's fame is the section called "Social Conditions as Shown in the Nights," which covers more than half of the essay. It contains four subsections: Al-Islam; women; pornography; and pederasty. In the section on Al-Islam, Burton discusses various religions, affirming that he was an adherent of none—"man never worshipped anything but himself." He calls the Old Testament an "immoral" work, and points out passages in the Bible containing "obscenity and impurity." In general he downgrades Christianity, but finds merit in the teachings of Mohammed, which he compares with those of Christianity, and he makes clear his preference for Al-Islam.

Burton then turns to the most notorious part of the essay: "Moslems and Easterns in general study and intelligently study the art and mystery of satisfying the physical woman." He lists several Arabian "classics" devoted to the subject, some of which he admits are "pornographic," and he reiterates his views about England's ignorance and stupidity: "It is said abroad that the English have the finest women in Europe and least know how to use them" (10:195–200).

In the section entitled "Pornography" Burton speaks of the "naive indecencies" of *The Arabian Nights'* text:

crude and indelicate with infantile plainness, even gross . . . but they cannot be accused of corrupting suggestiveness or subtle insinuation of vicious sentiment. Theirs is a coarseness of language, not of idea; they are indecent, not depraved; and the pure and perfect naturalness of their nudity seems almost to purify it, showing that the matter is rather of manners than of morals. . . . To those critics who complain of these raw vulgarisms and puerile indecencies in the *Nights* I can only reply by quoting the words said to have been said by Dr. Johnson to the lady who complained of the naughty words in his dictionary—"You must have been looking for them, Madam!" (10:203–4)

However, "there is another element in *The Arabian Nights* and that is one of absolute obscenity utterly repugnant to English readers, even the least prudish. It is chiefly connected with what our neighbors call *Le vice contre nature*—as if any thing can be contrary to nature which includes all things" (10:204). Nevertheless, Burton claims that on this subject he must offer details, "as it does not enter into my plan to ignore any theme which is interesting to the Orientalist and the Anthropologist. And they, methinks, do abundant harm who, for shame or disgust, would suppress the very mention of such matters: in order to combat a great and growing evil deadly to the birth-rate—the main-stay of national prosperity—the first requisite is careful study" (10:204). And he proclaims his intention to study it seriously, honestly, and historically, which he does in the next section on "Pederasty."

Burton begins with a brief recounting of his early report on the homosexual brothels in Karachi, which resulted, he believed, in his "summary dismissal from the service." In his many years of studying pederasty in various parts of the world, he became convinced that the practice was "geographic and climatic, not racial." After reminding his readers—"We must not forget that the love of boys has its noble sentimental side," Burton proceeds to give a scholarly survey of the subject—its history and geography. He establishes a geographical "Sotadic Zone" where pederasty is relatively common. It comprises essentially the world's temperate zone, spreading around the world at roughly the latitude of the Mediterranean. "Within the Sotadic Zone the Vice is popular and endemic, held at the worst to be a mere peccadillo, whilst the races to North and South of the limits here defined practise it only sporadically amid the opprobrium of their fellows . . ." (10:206–7).

Burton's historical discussion of pederasty, citing an impressive number of sources, begins with the Greeks and peoples of Asia Minor, and considers the role of pederasty in mythology and the Old Testament. He quotes from many scholars on the supposed physiological causes of "this pathological love, this perversion of the erotic sense" (10:209) and notes its role in the literature of the classical world. He describes the various forms the vice takes and its frequency in the Moslem world—even though it is expressly forbidden by the Koran—and compares the various regions of the Middle East with regard to their attitudes toward sex: the Turks, for example, being "born pederasts" (10:233).

While his discussion centers largely on masculine pederasty, he gives some attention to the forms homosexuality takes among women, and also the effect on wives and women in general when they are unfortunate enough to live in an area much given to male homosexuality: "We can hardly wonder at the loose conduct of Persian women perpetually mortified by marital pederasty." During periods when the British Bombay Army occupied regions in Persia, "even women of princely birth could not be kept out of the officers' quarters." In Afghanistan commercial caravans were invariably accompanied by "a number of boys and lads almost in women's attire with kohl'd eyes and rouged cheeks, long tresses and henna'd fingers and toes, riding luxuriously"—usually on camel-back. They are called "travelling wives, and the husbands trudge patiently by their sides." It is no surprise that in this country "a frantic debauchery broke out amongst the women when they found incubi who were not pederasts" (10:236).

Another result of the lack of heterosexuality in some regions was the prevalence, in harems and other such strictly female groups, of "every artifice of luxury . . . aphrodisiacs, erotic perfumes, singular applications" (what are often called today "marital aids")—devices and instruments designed to substitute for normal genitalia.

In writing on these subjects Burton drew extensively on his personal experience and knowledge but equally on an astonishing number of scholarly studies of those regions of which he lacked personal knowledge, such as the South Seas, Australia, and the Far East. He concludes his geographical and historical survey with a description of the role pederasty played in England and Western Europe during the seventeenth through the nineteenth centuries, especially in France. Much of this discussion, doubtless to the exasperation of most English readers, is conducted entirely in French (10:247–52).

Burton ends this section of the "Terminal Essay" by commenting on pederasty in *The Arabian Nights* themselves, which he divides into three categories: "The first is the funny form, as the unseemly practical joke of masterful Queen Budur (Vol. III, 300–306) and the not less *hardi* [bold] jest of the slave-princess Zumurrud (Vol. IV, 226). The second is in the grimmest and most earnest phase of the perversion, for instance where Abu Nowas debauches the three youths (Vol. V, 64–69); whilst in the third form it is wisely and learnedly discussed, to be severely banned, by the Shaykhah or Reverend Woman (Vol. V, 154)." Burton reminds the reader that, while "the Arab enjoys the startling and lively contrast of extreme virtue and horrible vice placed in juxtaposition . . . the proportion of offensive matter bears a very small ratio to the mass of the work" (10:252–53).

He also reminds the reader of the vulgar matter to be found in European classics—"Boccaccio and Chaucer, Shakespeare and Rabelais; [Robert] Burton, Stern, Swift and a long list of works which are yearly reprinted and republished without a word of protest"— to say nothing of the Old Testament with its "allusions to human ordure and the pudenda; to carnal copulation and impudent whoredom, to adultery and fornication, to onanism, sodomy and bestiality!" And he thanks the critic of the *Edinburgh Review* (a long-time enemy of Burton) for his "direct and deliberate falsehoods. . . . It appears to me that when I show to such men, so 'respectable' and so impure, a landscape of magnificient prospects whose vistas are adorned with every charm of nature and art, they point their unclean noses at a little heap of muck here and there lying in a field-corner" (10:254).

The last section of the essay is for linguistic scholars only: "On the Prose-Rhyme and the Poetry of the *Nights*"—a learned discussion of the language, grammar, and poetics of the tales, and the technical problems of translation (10:255–300).

In a brief "L'Envoi" Burton thanks the reader for his interest and patience; he admits to the possibility of his having made many errors, but contends that he has achieved, in his "labours of a quarter-century," what he set out to do: "to assist the student of Moslem life and of Arabo-Egyptian manners, customs and language in a multitude of matters shunned by books," to provide "a repertory of Eastern knowledge in its esoteric phase, sexual as well as social" (10:300).

Burton's *Arabian Nights* was unexpectedly both a critical and financial success. But in getting the work published Burton took certain risks. He was offended when a commercial publisher offered him only £500 for his translations, so he decided to publish them himself under the auspices of his Kama Shastra Society. They were to be printed privately with only 1,000 copies, to be sold by subscription at one guinea per volume. Burton was fearful at first that he would not get many subscribers, but the subscription list grew gradually to one thousand, then swelled to 2,000. He was pleasantly surprised but also bitter that he had not set his initial figure higher.

He spent 6,000 guineas in printing the sixteen volumes, and made a profit of 10,000 guineas. *The Arabian Nights* received considerable critical acclaim,[21] but the work was also—no doubt because of the "unexpurgated" translation, its candid footnotes, and its "Terminal Essay"—something of a *succès de scandale*. The fact that it was the center of a heated controversy, as well as its literary merits, probably served to recommend it to many subscribers. He wrote ironically: "I struggled for forty-seven years. I distinguished myself honorably in every way I possibly could. I never had a compliment nor a 'Thank you,' nor a single farthing. I translated a doubtful book in my old age, and immediately made sixteen thousand guineas. Now that I know the tastes of England, we need never to be without money."[22]

Chapter Seven
Exotic Erotica

Sexuality: The Victorian Viewpoint

From 1873 until his death in 1890 Burton was engaged in secret printing of erotica, which could have put him in serious trouble with the law. He could have been prosecuted under the Obscene Publications Act of 1857; and the Society for the Suppression of Vice was very busy, having charged and gained convictions of hundreds of authors of whose works the Society disapproved. Interestingly enough, the reading public, and apparently the Society, tolerated Burton's accounts of the sexual habits of the Africans and American Indians, probably because they dealt with "savages." But even there Burton had to be careful. In his early works he put much dangerous material in Latin footnotes, or suffered having them deleted completely, and he avoided discussing the sexual act itself. He had to be especially careful in dealing with female sexuality, for this was an era in which the British public agreed with the eminent physician Dr. William Acton, whose widely read books affirmed that "the majority of women (happily for society) are not very much troubled with sexual feeling of any kind."[1]

Burton, then, was writing at the height of a period when ignorance, which took the form of suppression, distortion, and repression, dominated the English understanding of sexuality. Appalled at the damage to human life caused by this ignorance, he was determined to bring some light to the subject. He pointed out that the average educated Englishwoman, far from living without sexual feelings, lived "in a rustle of (imaginary) copulation." Women of primitive societies could "relieve the brain through the body," but the English-woman had to turn instead to fantasies and to reading French novels—"visions amatory and venereal"—many of which were officially banned. Many women, he insisted, turn to "some counter-agent—religion, pride, or physical frigidity." He reminded his readers that frequently a woman, even one of the upper classes, "when stricken by insanity or puerperal fever, breaks out into language that would shame the slums and which makes the hearers marvel where she could have learned such vocabulary. How many an old maid held to be as cold as virgin snow, and how many a matron upon whose fairest fame not a breath of scandal has blown, how many a widow who proudly claims the title *univira* [chaste widow] must relieve their pent-up feelings by what may be called mental prostitution."[2]

For years Burton had raged against the prohibitions that prevented the full use of his knowledge, of the rich materials in his vast storehouse of folklore and literature of Oriental wisdom on love; thus during the last seventeen years of his life he decided to fling open the gates of that "stream dammed up with mud." The most barbarous tribes of Africa, Australia, and the Americas, he claimed, educate their boys at puberty in "the 'theorick and practick' of social and sexual relations. Amongst the civilised this fruit of the knowledge-tree must be bought at the price of the bitterest experience, and the consequences of ignorance are peculiarly cruel."[3] These cruel consequences are especially destructive among women of Western Europe:

How often do we hear women in Society lamenting that they have absolutely no knowledge of their own physiology; and at what heavy price must this fruit of the knowledge-tree be bought by the young first entering life. Shall we ever understand that ignorance is not innocence? . . . She has feet but no "toes"; ankles but no "calves"; knees but no "thighs"; a stomach but no "belly" nor "bowels"; hips and no "haunches"; a bust but no "backside" nor "buttocks"; in fact, she is a monstrum, a figure only to frighten the crows. . . . Respectability unmakes what nature made. . . .

Moslems and Easterns in general study and intelligently study the art and mystery of satisfying the physical woman. . . . The mock virtue, the most immodest modesty of England and of the United States in the sixth century, pronounces the subject foul and fulsome: "Society" sickens at all details; and hence it is said abroad that the English have the finest women in Europe and least know how to use them. Throughout the East such studies are aided by a long series of volumes, many of them written by learned physiologists, by men of social standing and by religious dignitaries in high office. . . .[4]

When not fulminating against Victorian abhorrence of sex, he was making jokes about it. He was fond of repeating the story of "the chloroformed bride upon whose pillow the bridegroom found a paper pinned and containing the words, 'Mama says you're to do what you like.' "[5]

Burton's writings on sexuality appear in three different forms: first, they are scattered throughout his various travel books on Africa, the Middle East and India, and the Americas; second, he published several translations of books devoted exclusively to the "art of love"; and third, other and later writers helped themselves generously to Burton's writings and produced books drawn entirely, or almost entirely, from Burton.[6] In his travel books Burton showed an obsessive interest in sexuality and depicted, as frankly as his publishers would permit, the details of sexual life in every region he visited. But some of these writings could scarcely be called "erotic"—his many descriptions of circumcision rites and clitorectomy, infibulation, the making of eunuchs, and various other practices of sexual mutilation could be seen by most readers as decidedly anti-erotic, though it is apparent that Burton found such matters to be fascinating.

The Translations: East Indian Erotica

Burton's first translation of Eastern erotica was the *Ananga Ranga,* a Hindu manual of explicit directions on the art of making love, which he finished in 1873. He gave it a different name, however, the *Kama Shastra,* and provided on the title page the following elaborate description: "Kama Shastra or the Hindoo Art of Love (Ars Amoris Indica) Translated from the Sanscrit and Annotated by A. F. F. and B. F. R. For the Private Use of the Translators Only in Connection with a Work on the Hindoo Religion, and on the Manners and Customs of the Hindoos." The initials of the two translators are those of Arbuthnot and Burton printed backward, an indication of their nervousness at bringing out such a dangerous book. But they needed not have taken such precautions, as the book was not published. The printer, on reading the proofs, became alarmed at the contents and refused to print it. Years later, in 1885, with a more courageous printer, the work was finally published under the auspices of the Kama Shastra Society and bore the title of *Ananga Ranga.*[7] In addition to this work and the *Arabian Nights,* the Society published four other Eastern volumes: the *Kama Sutra* (1883) translated by Burton and Arbuthnot; and *The Perfumed Garden of the Cheikh Nefzaoui, A Manuel of Arabic Erotology (xiv Century)* (1886) translated by Burton alone. *Beharistan* (1887) and *Gulistan* (1888) were thought to have been translated by Burton but apparently he merely supervised the translation which was actually done by Edward Rehatsek, a friend of Burton and Arbuthnot who had spent most of his life in India.

Ananga Ranga

The *Ananga Ranga* (1885)[8] begins with an introduction in which the reader is told: "And thus all of you who read this book shall know how delicious an instrument is woman, when artfully played upon; how capable she is of producing the most exquisite harmony; of executing the most complicated variations and of giving the divinist pleasures" (xxiii). The aim of the book is clearly stated: how to avoid the causes for separation of married couples due to monotony—"how the husband, by varying the enjoyment of his wife, may live with her as with thirty-two different women, ever varying the enjoyment of her, and rendering satiety impossible" (129). To help the man and woman to achieve this desired bliss, the book offers a plenitude of sexual approaches, techniques, and positions, with charts and diagrams, and lists of aphrodisiacs, ointments, and foods conducive to sexual prowess. The book also includes many photographs of Indian erotic statuary and temple carvings.

The translation by Burton and Arbuthnot is rendered in a matter-of-fact style, as is appropriate for a work intended to be serious and in no way sensational. It begins by classifying various types of men and women, usually into groups according to geographical region, all the people in those regions presumably possessing certain characteristics in common. The chapter titles give some idea of the contents: "Of the Four Orders of Woman"; "Of the Various Sorts of Passion in Women"; "Of the Different Kinds of Men and Women"; "Description of the General Qualities, Characteristics, Temperaments of Women"; "Characteristics of Women of Various Lands"; "On Useful Medicines"; "Treating of Vashikaran, or the Art of Fascination by Use of Charms"; "On Different Signs in Men and Women"; "Treating of External Enjoyments"; "Treating of Internal Enjoyments." By "external enjoyments" is meant "the process which should precede internal enjoyment or coition," that is, "eight modes of embraces" or what is popularly known as foreplay. By "internal enjoyments" is meant "the art of congress which follows the various external preliminaries," that is, divisions and subdivisions of love-making positions.

All of this solemn numerical advice is interesting enough to the Western reader, but also very foreign to Western notions of love-making and at times even humorous. Burton and Arbuthnot are aware of this; they state in the preface that the book possesses "a peculiar quaintness, resulting from the language and from the pe-culiarities of Hindu thought. . . . Nothing can be more charac-teristic of the Indian than this laboured and mechanical style of love; when kisses are divided into so many kinds; when there are rules for patting with the palm and the back of the hand, and regulations for the several expirations of breath. Regarded in this light, the book becomes an ethnological treasure . . ." (viii).

However strange the work might appear to Europeans, it was extremely popular in the East. The translators claim that the *Ananga Ranga* had been translated into most all Eastern languages—hundreds of thousands of copies—and "the book is in the hands of both sexes and all ages throughout the nearer East, and possibly it may extend to China and Japan" (xii).

It is also important to realize that the book has dimensions other than the physically erotic. The original author, Kalyana Malla, is described as being "devout and highly moral." The reader is re-minded that "every stanza of the work has a double signification, after the fashion of the Vedanta, and may be interpreted in two ways, either mystical or amatory" (xxiii). This religious aspect is also stressed by the several scholars whose commentaries on the illustrations of Indian sculpture appear in the introductory part of the book. As Coomaraswamy says in his comments: "in nearly all Indian art there runs a vein of deep sex-mysticism. Not only are female forms felt to be equally appropriate with the male to ad-umbrate the majesty of the Over-Soul, but the interplay of all psychic and physical sexual forces is felt in itself to be religious" (xvi). This element of the work is usually not understood or is overlooked entirely by Western critics and, for that matter, booksellers and buyers, who saw the book simply as pornography.

The Kama Sutra

The next work of Eastern erotica to be translated by Burton, also

in collaboration with F. F. Arbuthnot, was the *Kama Sutra* (1883).[9]
It also has achieved some notoriety among Western readers as a
rather spicy treatise on sex, but, like the *Ananga Ranga,* it was
produced in the spirit of piety and moral edification. Written in
Sanskrit sometime between the first and fourth centuries A.D., it
was, according to one Indian scholar, "composed according to the
precepts of the Holy Writ, for the benefit of the world, by Vatsyayana, while leading the life of a religious student and wholly
engaged in the contemplation of the Deity. . . . Sex is not only
considered normal and necessary but almost sacramental."[10]

The work is written, as its name indicates, in *sutra* form, that
is, in aphorisms. Thus "kama sutra" means aphorisms on love or
the life of the senses. But any reader seeking to find "pornography"
in the book will be disappointed. Only a small part deals explicitly
with the sex act, but even there the author's attitude, like Burton's,
is that of the moralist. Even in passages devoted to describing various
phases of physical love, Vatsyayana is careful to point out that though
particular practices are described in books there is no reason they
should actively be tried. The author's attitude and approach is essentially that of a sociologist: he puts emphasis on the habits and
customs of different regions of India, and he insists that sex must
be seen as only one part of a large and complex social system: "This
work is not to be used merely as an instrument for satisfying our
desires. A person, acquainted with the true principles of this science,
and who preserves his Dharma, Artha, and Kama is sure to gain
mastery over his senses."[11] That is, one must study all the arts of
life in addition to that of the senses. True "kama" will be achieved
only when it follows intellectual achievements (such as mathematics,
chemistry, architecture, etc.) and aesthetic achievements (such as
music, painting, dance—the author lists sixty-four activities in all).
Literature, art, dance, and music are especially important studies—
"a man should have a cultivated mind and body, with intellectual
and artistic interests, if he is to lead a proper and disciplined life
of enjoyment."[12]

The *Kama Sutra* is similar to the *Ananga Ranga* in its style and
organization. The many activities generally related to the art of
living as well as the art of love are classified, divided, subdivided,
and labeled with their own unique names. First, one finds types of
men and women classified according to the size of their genitalia,

as Hares, Bulls, or Horses (men) or as Deer, Mares, or Elephants (women), and the appropriate match-ups are prescribed. Similarly, their degrees of "passion" are identified (87–88). Various "embraces" are defined: touching, piercing, rubbing, and pressing, as are the types of kissing: "the normal kiss," "the throbbing kiss," "the touching kiss," "the straight kiss," "the bent kiss," "the turned kiss," and "the pressed kiss" (93–101).

One aspect of the author's advice, which was undoubtedly of interest to Burton, is his treatment of pain, which he holds to be an important part of pleasure, and so he includes descriptions of striking, biting, and scratching, and gives each gesture its various modes—for example, eight ways of pressing with the fingernails, which themselves are divided into small, middling, and large. The preferred kind of teeth are also described, those which can best execute the "hidden bite" and "the swollen bite," and those bites decoratively called the "coral and the jewel" and "the broken cloud" (102). Similarly, one learns of "the various modes of striking and of the sounds appropriate to them" (110–12).

The various positions for the sex act are then briefly portrayed, many of them being highly imaginative, even acrobatic; and types of "mouth congress" (oral sex) are defined, also briefly (106–9, 116–19).

The next part treats of courtship, marriage, and other social institutions. Marriage is usually arranged in Indian culture, but here the author insists that "no other girl than the one who is loved should be married." He explains the need for "mutual confidence" in marriage, and gives suggestions for courtship, emphasizing gentleness, tenderness, thoughtfulness, and other such desirable traits. Thus the *Kama Sutra* is a book on the whole art of love, not just sexual relations. And here is where it differs from such works as Ovid's *Art of Love*. Ovid was writing, for men only, a text on successful seduction and the experiencing of pleasure. The *Kama Sutra* addresses itself to women as well as men and is concerned with the whole life. It gives women much practical advice on such matters as their wifely duties and how to ensure conjugal happiness.

Burton intended that the *Kama Sutra* would prove enlightening and beneficial to its English readers, enriching life and helping to avoid the miseries and failures caused by sexual ignorance and prejudice. He was aware, however, that as a practical handbook of guidance in amatory affairs, the work left much to be desired. As has been pointed out by more than one commentator, the book introduces its readers to coital positions, sexual techniques, and physical "improvements" far too "acrobatic," bizarre, and in some cases downright dangerous, to be of great value. Nevertheless, the work may well have served Burton's purpose: its contents and attitudes probably administered a necessary shock to its nineteenth-century audience and served to widen current ideas of the possibilities of sex, even if no one in the present century would turn to the *Kama Sutra* for serious instruction. There are many more modern works which contain information more relevant to contemporary Western life than Vatsyayana's ancient classic—though it is very probable that the *Kama Sutra,* and Burton's good work in translating it, made possible the production and favorable reception of those later works. As with most all of his writings about the East, Burton wanted to dispel the prevailing Western ignorance, and modern scholars are surely correct when they see the importance of the *Kama Sutra* (and of the other books discussed in this chapter) in its being the expression and explanation of fundamental Indian values and beliefs: "It revolutionized the Western approach to Indian culture. It showed how central and natural sex was to Indian thought and life. Indian art, poetry and religion had all reflected this basic concern. It is not too much to claim that from this classic translation in 1883 the modern understanding of Indian art and culture derives."[13]

In translating the most explicit passages, Burton and Arbuthnot strove to avoid any taint of obscenity. They chose the most delicate and neutral language, and throughout they used the Hindu words for the sexual organs: yoni and lingam. When the book was formally published in England and the United States, reviewers expressed surprise that it should for so many decades have been considered pornographic. The public should be grateful, one reviewer proclaimed, "that after whole forests have been felled to publicize a modern rediscovery of the female orgasm we can have the matter settled in a classical dissertation of six pages.[14]

The Translations: Italian and Latin Erotica

After finishing the six volumes of the *Supplemental Nights* in 1888, Burton decided to translate an unexpurgated version of Boccaccio's *Decameron,* but he discovered that (once again) Payne had already produced one, so he shifted to a collection of earthy Neapolitan folktales, *Il Pentamerone, or the Tales of Tales* by Giovanni Batiste Basile (written in 1637).[15] This work, published posthumously in 1893 in a subscriber's edition of 1,500 copies, turned out to be one of Burton's more successful translations. This collection of tales does not qualify as true "erotica"—rather it is earthy and bawdy and gave Burton the opportunity to use his extensive knowledge of the Neapolitan street language he had acquired during his youth.

These tales, like those of Boccaccio, have a strong Eastern flavor. In many respects—in their rich combining of realism and fantasy, magic, the supernatural, romance and violence—they resemble the tales in *The Arabian Nights*. It is for this reason, no doubt, that Burton was so suitable a translator of the *Pentamerone*. Fresh from his translation of *The Arabian Nights* Burton's style kept "the flourishes and hyperboles of the East." According to some experts on the Neapolitan language, Burton often misunderstood difficult Neapolitan words and phrases, and his English is, as usual, most odd, but there is general agreement that the stories flow smoothly and that the curious style seems suited to the curious matter.[16]

Burton also decided that certain Italian and Latin poets, most of whose works were well known, should be more fully translated. He resolved to work on those verses usually omitted from standard editions as being too obscene or perverse for general consumption—writings of Ariosto, Apuleius, Catullus, and Juvenal. In this enterprise he chose to collaborate with Leonard Smithers, a young English solicitor who spent his leisure hours in collecting and translating erotica. Smithers, who was to acquire a reputation in London literary circles as an "erotic specialist," had rendered into English prose a number of poems from the Latin *Priapeia,* a notorious collection of explicit verses about the god Priapus, who was usually depicted as possessing a giant penis in constant erection. Burton never met Smithers, but they communicated by mail, and eventually brought out (1889) a three-part volume containing the original Latin, Smithers's prose, and Burton's verse translations. They used the pseudonyms Outidanos and Neaniskos, and the work was printed under the auspices of the so-called Erotika Biblion Society, presumably located in Athens. Smithers, perhaps naively, was completely unafraid of being prosecuted under the Obscenity Act; he wanted to bring out a second edition under their right names, but Burton, after Isabel created a considerable fuss,[17] decided against the daring plan, and so the second edition appeared in 1890 under the original pseudonyms.

The Translations: Arabian Erotica

Burton then worked for a time translating Ariosto, Apuleius, and Ausonius, but these he abandoned in order to translate *The Perfumed Garden of the Cheikh Nefzaoui, A Manual of Arabic Erotology (vxi Century)*. It was published by the Kama Shastra Society in 1886 for private circulation only. This edition, which Burton had produced from a French translation, was soon sold out. He then decided to by-pass the French version and seek out the original Arabic manuscript, with the intention of retranslating it as *The Scented Garden*. It was to be an enlarged and annotated edition including a chapter on homosexuality, which was previously omitted, and some new material on Chinese eunuchs. These two themes, homosexuality, and eunuchs, apparently obsessed Burton, as he returned to them repeatedly in his various books, much to his wife's distress. This new translation, however, never reached the printers. Burton died while working on it, and it was included among the papers that Isabel burned. But while he lived, Burton was convinced of the importance and value of his new translation: "I have put my whole life and all my life-blood into that *Scented Garden;* it is my great hope that I shall live by it. It is the crown of my life.[18] But Isabel, in her violent opposition to the book, considered it to be primarily concerned with sexual perversities, whereas in fact it was a manual of definitely heterosexual love with only the last chapter and certain notes dealing with homosexuality.[19]

The Perfumed Garden of Shaykh Nefzawi

The origins of *The Perfumed Garden* (1886)[20] are obscure: it is said to have been written by a sixteenth-century "shaykh" whose name appears in the title. Its contents are similar to those of the *Kama Sutra* and the *Ananga Ranga*—solemn advice that treats its subject in a reverential manner, believing it to be a natural and necessary part of the divine design. Its main difference from the *Kama Sutra* is that the *Garden* is ornamented with legends, folktales, and anecdotes illustrative of the subject matter of the text. One of its main similarities is that it includes a section devoted to the deceits and treacheries of women in matters of love. These stories are remarkably similar in content and style to many of those in the *Arabian Nights,* and may be drawn from the same sources.[21] In its purpose, which had Burton's complete approval, the *Garden* is comparable to the *Ananga Ranga:* to increase the pleasure and joy of the sex act, to assist men and women to avoid monotony and satiety, so that partners in love may continue to perform as if young and freshly in love. Much attention is given to *Imsak*—the special art of delaying the male climax and prolonging the sex act. Burton tells us, in a different context, that "Europeans ignoring the science are contemptuously compared with village-cocks by Hindu women."[22]

Just as in its Indian counterpart, the Arabic manual is divided into various chapters offering advice on the physical aspects of lovemaking: positions and conditions conducive to satisfactory performance, including some considerate suggestions for the physically deformed or impaired; diets and recipes, some of which seem like magic potions, that would help one overcome sexual deficiencies; descriptions of what kind of men make appropriate partners for what kind of woman, and vice-versa; medical advice, concoctions, ointments, herbs, and such, to help cure various sexual disfunctions— all of which must appear bizarre, even ridiculous, to the modern Western reader—along with some good commonsense advice: when "approaching the woman, you should not have your stomach loaded with food and drink"; and after making love, "be careful not to get up at once. . . . remain close to the woman" and do not be in a haste to leave (126).

And then there is the inevitable "On the Deceits and Treacheries of Women" presented in six illustrative stories, which are introduced by a supporting quotation from the *Koran:* "the strategems of women are numerous and ingenious. Their tricks will deceive Satan himself, for God, the Highest, has said (*Koran,* VI, verse 28) that the deceptive faculties of women are great, and he has likewise said (*Koran,* VI, verse 38) that the strategems of Satan are weak. Comparing the word of God as to the ruses of Satan and women, contained in those two verses, it is easy to see how great these latter ones are" (208).

The original French translator of the *Garden* added an appendix, "To the Reader," which included some observations with which Burton must surely have agreed. For example, the admission that "the work is encumbered with a quantity of matter which cannot but appear ridiculous in the eyes of the civilized modern reader; but we should not have been justified in weeding it out. . . . Those

oddities are, moreover, instructive, as they make us acquainted with
the manner and character of the Arab under a peculiar aspect, and
not only of the Arab who was contemporary with our author Nefzawi.
The latter is, in fact, not much more advanced than the former."
Many of these "ridiculous notions" continue into the present day.
"With the Arab, probability is frequently sacrificed to imagination"
(270–71).

Burton's Erotica: Its Value and Influence

What, ultimately, is the value of these works of Eastern erotica
on which Burton lavished a lifetime's accumulation of knowledge
of exotic customs, attitudes, and languages? It was Burton's stated
hope, as we have seen, to bring enlightenment to the prudish Western world, England in particular, and to alleviate suffering and
provide happiness in matters of sexual relationships. But it is apparent, and usually conceded by both Burton and other scholars,
that the sexual practices so solemnly advocated by the East were
scarcely adaptable to the culture of the West. But Burton added
another value to be gained from these works, which he placed in
the realm of folklore—useful knowledge of Eastern beliefs and values, of the "Oriental mind," which might aid the West in its need
to establish a comfortable rapport with the Eastern countries. But
the principal value of Burton's translations is found in an area which
he probably foresaw: his work was enormously influential in that it
broke down barriers and opened the way to a more enlightened
study of sexuality, even if the Eastern works themselves did not
provide that enlightenment. First of all, as they gained acceptance,
the *Ananga Ranga,* the *Kama Sutra,* and the *Perfumed Garden* exemplified an attitude and a methodology. The attitude was one of
openness, objectivity, and candor in admitting the study and knowledge of sexuality into respectable company with other social sciences.
Some observers see Vatsyayana *(Kama Sutra)* as the forerunner of the
"sociological" approaches of such pioneer researchers as Havelock
Ellis, Malinowski, and Kraft-Ebbing, all of whom, like Vatsyayana,
dealt objectively with the intimate aspects of sexuality placed in a
broad social setting.

One recent scholar is emphatic on the subject of Burton's influence
on subsequent researchers of human sexuality: "Almost throughout
his life Burton had been extremely interested in the subject of

homosexuality. He may be considered, in fact, the pioneer in the serious study of this subject in England; for, without doubt, he paved the way for that classic volume which forms the second part of Havelock Ellis's monumental *Studies in the Psychology of Sex* [i.e., *Sexual Inversion* (1897)].[23]

However, as we have pointed out, while Burton did evince a lively interest in such matters as homosexuality and eunuchs, the three classic works under consideration here were primarily concerned with heterosexual relations within the context of marriage. There is little doubt that many of the innumerable authors of popular volumes of sex instruction owe some of their methodology to the writings of Vatsyayana *(Kama Sutra)*, Shaykh Nefzawi *(Perfumed Garden)*, and Kalyana Malla *(Ananga Ranga)* in Burton's translations. They likewise owe some of their information to the copious notes and profoundly informed annotations to Burton's *Arabian Nights*. And the most distinguished of these authors have clearly stated their sources. Havelock Ellis, for example, refers to and quotes Burton's translation of Nefzawi in his *Studies in the Psychology of Sex;* Kinsey does likewise in his *Sexual Behavior in the Human Male;* and Norman Hines included *The Perfumed Garden* among the Arabic sources utilized when writing his *Medical History of Contraception* (1936). "This list could be extended, but it seems a trifle unnecessary to state the obvious."[24]

It has been eloquently pointed out that for "this dispersal of fogs of ignorance, the imparting of sound techniques accompanied by a healthy mental attitude, and the inculcation of a confidence productive of happiness and (for their respective religions) self-respect," one must be grateful to Burton for his labors and learning in translating these three Eastern classics, which have become "Beacons shining from the past and illuminating the future—a guiding light which can be seen, quietly Christianised and modified for occidental use, in not a few of the authoritative, scientific, and even popular treatises of our century."[25] A bit rhapsodically expressed, perhaps, but these views accurately sum up the influence and significance of Burton's translations and annotations in the contemporary study of human sexuality.

Chapter Eight
Burton: The Man and the Writer

When Burton died in 1890, the many obituaries that appeared were for the most part positive, the writers of these notices coming to his defense for a variety of reasons: outrage at Isabel Burton's destruction of her husband's manuscripts; the strong sense that Burton's achievements had not been properly recognized and rewarded by British officialdom; and a genuine admiration for the man himself. He was praised for his contributions to the new sciences of anthropology and ethnology, for his awesome energy which resulted in his collecting and classifying "an incredible mass of fascinating and often obscure facts and information, his insatiable curiosity which led him to explore almost every path of learning, especially the by-paths."[1] He wrote forty-three volumes about his explorations and travels, of which the *Pilgrimage to Al-Madinah and Meccah* and *The Lake Regions of Central Africa* are recognized classics. Also receiving special praise are *First Footsteps in East Africa* and *City of the Saints,* which has been described as the best book on the Mormons published in the nineteenth century.[2] In the field of archeology Burton was admittedly a dilettante, but as a linguist and translator his reputation seems secure. He not only mastered twenty-five languages along with another fifteen dialects, but he compiled vocabularies of little known languages wherever he found them, for the benefit of travelers who would follow him.

In the end it was undoubtedly translation that was his most satisfying work—translation which for all its flaws possessed the integrity, brilliance, and vigor of the man himself. He moved with astonishing ease from the Hindustani of *Vikram and the Vampire,* to Portuguese for Camoens's *Lusiads,* to Arabic for *The Arabian Nights* and *The Perfumed Garden,* to Neapolitan Italian for *Il Pentamerone,* to Sanskrit for the *Kama Sutra* and *Ananga Ranga,* and to Latin for his *Priapeia* and Catullus. For these achievements, as well as his travel books, Burton has been justly admired; but the same writers who praised him could also misjudge him, claiming, for example, that "his cast of mind was so original that not only did he not borrow from anyone else, but he was disposed to resent another's trespassing upon such subjects as he considered his own."[3] To the contrary, Burton was not especially "original" in his attitudes and beliefs, and he was openly generous in his crediting his predecessors and fellow explorers. He read and quoted all works he could find that antedated his own, and, with the notable exception of his personal quarrel with John Speke regarding the headwaters of the Nile, he was always ready to give credit where due, and to assist, from the stores of his own knowledge and experience, young explorers and scholars who sought his advice. And to those who were admitted to his intimacy, "the man was greater than what he did or what he wrote."

This last notion, that the man was greater than his works, has been expressed by a number of critics: it is implicit in recent biographies and flatly stated by Alan Moorehead and Fawn Brodie, and it invites further consideration of just who and what was the "man himself." Since the present study is concerned with Burton as a writer, it is through his published works that we must see and judge him—works that have provoked persistent questions about Burton's character. There are some recurrent themes that run through Burton's writings which, while not diminishing the magnitude of his achievement, serve to call into question in some critics' minds the authenticity and value of many of these writings: Burton's blatant racism, and his obsession with the more sensational aspects of sexuality. Another trait that characterizes Burton's life and writing was his penchant for disguise, for assuming roles, which had a marked effect on his literary work.

From the time he was a teenager, when he assumed the role of *croquemort* in order to participate in the collecting and burial of cholera victims in Naples, Burton delighted in theatrical disguises. Sometimes in costume—as a Persian merchant in India, an Indian doctor in Egypt and Arabia, and Moslem merchant in Somaliland— and sometimes without costume, he assumed and shed new roles up to his death, including such diverse roles as soldier, swordsman, explorer, anthropologist, archeologist, mining speculator, responsible consul, man about town, Arab sheikh, and, in between, devoted husband. He brought to all these roles his characteristic courage, enthusiasm, energy, and dramatic posturings, along with earnestness and exhaustive scholarship. But it is no doubt true that "the wild diversity of these roles served also to obscure the real man and the nature of the 'demon' that drove him from one to another."[4] Each of his books, whatever else it was about, reveals him testing a new identity.

Burton's early books of travel show him frankly searching for fame as a pioneering explorer; he then sought renown as a scientist and scholar; and ultimately he claimed the world's admiration through his translations and personal writings. But throughout his life, despite his many successes, he seems to have suffered from depression, anguish, and guilt. His books, especially those he wrote and translated in his later years, suggest that he sought in the amassing of facts about human relationships, love, and sexuality a compensation for the apparent failures of his personal life. In matters of sexual relations, as in most everything else in his life, he fled from the conventional and the sanctioned; he was drawn to the exotic and forbidden. His writings indicate that he once had an Indian mistress, that he had a brief passionate affair with a Persian woman, and even made an abortive attempt at seducing a nun. His travel books contain strong hints about sexual experiences with the women of Africa. All of this seems "normal" enough, but what has bothered many of Burton's critics has been his repeated emphasis on what they considered unsavory aspects of sexuality—how eunuchs become eunuchs, bizarre and often sadistic circumcisions, clitorectomies, and other mutilation rites, and the fact that he probably wrote more extensively than any other man of his time about pederasty.

There is no question that Burton's work in providing translations of Eastern erotica has had an important effect on subsequent writing on the subject. Twentieth-century scholars on the subject have acknowledged Burton's pioneering and generally salutary contributions to candid and more accurate information about human relations.[5] Another central aspect of his writing is equally important but more subject to controversy: the "image" of the African and the "Oriental" (meaning in Burton's case the people of India and the Near East) that emerges strongly from Burton's travel books.

Burton's writings on India and Arabia did much to create the image of the Middle Eastern "Oriental" in nineteenth-century British minds. It is a blurred image, however, due in part to Burton's inability, as we have seen, to sustain a consistent point of view. For Burton, as some of his biographers and commentators have observed, was a curiously "divided" man. But then most British travelers who wrote of India and the Middle East were divided in some important sense, and it is the special form of their individual inner conflicts that creates the quality which distinguishes their writings as literature. Indeed, recent studies of travel writing tend to view such works not so much as sources of information about the countries visited as revelations of the unique sensibility and values of the writer and his culture. Just as Charles Doughty's view of *Arabia Deserta* (1888) was conditioned by his love of the English past, and as Wilfrid Blunt's anti-imperialism reflects a tension between practical politics and a thoroughly romantic conception of the East, so Burton's writings reveal a man struggling with, and usually failing to resolve, many personal tensions which determined his reactions to the Orient. An examination of these inner conflicts shows Burton to be a man without a firm personal and cultural position from which to view and judge other cultures. He never discovered who or what he was himself, and so his views of others remain inconsistent and contradictory. Only in his two works on Arabia—*Pilgrimage* and *The Arabian Nights*—did he so involve himself in Al-Islam, with imagination and sympathetic insight, as to create works of relative coherence and literary quality. Only when in successful Moslem disguise and enjoying total acceptance in the Islamic world did Burton approach a degree of respite from his painfully divided nature. But even there, as we have seen, the divisions remained.

This "divided Burton" is probably to a great extent the cause of the divided criticism his books have received. From the time his works began to appear in the 1850s to the present, opinion has been sharply divided as to the quality of Burton's writing and the accuracy of his portrayal of African and Eastern peoples and cultures. One of his better biographers thinks that Burton's four books on India were just thrown together without regard for organization or "appropriateness" and are filled with "literary and philosophical rubbish."[6] One of his other biographers, however, considers Burton's two books on the Indian province of Sind to be "solid brilliant ethnological studies,"[7] as does the English scholar who edited one of his books on Sind.[8] And regarding Burton's main book on Arabia, *Pilgrimage,* opinions are equally divided. While *Pilgrimage* shows considerable improvement over the India books, the writing is unequal in quality and has led some critics to deplore his lack of literary talent. An anonymous contemporary reviewer criticized *Pil-*

grimage for its "levelness of recital which brings the more momentous passages upon the reader suddenly as if he had collided with someone in turning a corner."[9] One of his admirers admitted that Burton "was a man of genius; only, the fact is, he is not a great writer. . . . There can be no doubt that Burton always gives a vivid and virile impression of his adventures; yet, as I have said before, something is lacking in his prose; not the vital heat, but the vision of what is equivalent to vital heat."[10]

Two authors who have special qualifications for judging Burton's works also expressed contrary views. T. E. Lawrence does not say much directly about Burton's style, but makes his judgment evident by indirect means. In his letters and prefaces he indicates his preferences among earlier travel writers, and he makes it clear that he judged travel books primarily on what he considered to be their literary quality. Here Burton did not score very well. Lawrence refers infrequently to Burton, indicating a "disapproving literary rather than scientific judgment." On the other hand, Lawrence greatly admired Doughty's *Travels in Arabia Deserta* and Kinglake's *Eothen*. Doughty's book was "a work of art": "Its value doesn't lie in its exactness to life in Arabia (on which I can pose as an authority), but on its goodness as writing."[11] Alan Moorehead, however, sees Burton's literary abilities differently. Commenting on his books on Africa, Moorehead says that Burton "is a natural writer. He feels at ease with his pen just as other men are at ease in their conversation. Similes, witticisms, flights of imagination, scientific speculations and historical theories pour out of him in a babbling irrepressible stream. The language is Johnsonian, the tone is by turns ironic, boistrous, pedantic, argumentative, and just occasionally downright sardonic."[12]

Critics have also been unable to agree on the accuracy of Burton's portrayal of the East and of his understanding of the Middle Eastern mind. One biographer says flatly that Burton failed utterly to comprehend the Arab's character and psychology,[13] whereas another says that of the various writers on Arabia—Blunt, Doughty, Lawrence, Palgrave, Burton—only Burton solved "the riddle of the Arab," only he "saw eye to eye with the Arab."[14] In one perceptive study of Burton, Blunt, and Doughty, a scholar points out that these three travelers, with differing feelings about British imperialism and differing temperaments, "came to three different views, each of which was thought to be the proper understanding of the Arab world." It is all too easy, he says, to point out the limitations of these views (he thought Burton's picture of the Arab was "too grotesque") and that "it is much more difficult to understand the temperaments and sensibilities which made these views so colorful; but the attempt is extremely rewarding in that it involves three fascinating men in an extremely lively period in human history."[15]

Another writer describes all three of these travelers, Burton, Blunt, and Doughty, as "dangerous guides" to the cultures of the Arabian deserts, because they all—even Burton who is acknowledged to be an accomplished Orientalist—wrote a species of "fiction": their works are primarily works of the imagination, carrying on, consciously or not, the romantic literary traditions of *The Arabian Nights*.[16] Edward Said, picking up on these arguments and working straight out of Thomas Assad (whom he cites), claims that Burton, as narrator and "principal character" of his books, was as much "the center of fantastic adventure and even fantasy as the authoritative commentator and detached Westerner on Oriental society and customs." He sees Burton as the first in a series of "fiercely individualistic Victorian travelers in the East" but adds that "Burton's legacy is more complex than individualistic precisely because in his writings we can find exemplified the struggle between individualism and a strong feeling of national identification with Europe (specifically England) as an imperial power in the East." For all Burton's sympathetic self-association with the Arabs, he was nevertheless, and always, the imperialist. But what is most relevant, according to Said, is that "Burton thought of himself both as a rebel against authority (hence his identification with the East as a place of freedom from Victorian moral authority) and as a potential agent of authority in the East. It is the manner of that coexistence, between two antagonistic roles for himself, that is of interest."[17]

Whatever these critics may have thought of Burton's qualities as writer and observer, they all agree on the central point emerging here: that Burton was a curious and complex man whose writings reflect an interestingly divided nature. It is apparent, when one considers his biography, that Burton's conflicting attitudes toward other societies and races have their roots in his own early life. Since he never really had a home, he never identified closely with any society. He spent his childhood years wandering with his family in southern France and Italy, speaking the local languages and absorbing the local cultures. He returned to England only when he had to, and, on the occasions he was obliged to spend some time among his countrymen, he almost always alienated them. When in "respectable" company he usually said the very things most likely to shock and offend his listeners, and he preferred the company of the bohemian literary fringes of society. After being thrown out of Oxford University and shipping out to India as an officer in the Bombay Army, he offended most of his fellow officers and superiors and sought the company of the native Indians. As he gained in knowledge and expertise, he became increasingly critical of the English military and civil service, constantly pointing out their ignorance of Indian culture and ineptitude in dealing with the peoples they were supposed to govern. But he could also irritate the Indians, when he wrote his books, with his condescension, his undisguised sense of white English superiority, and tendency to refer to the darker races as barbarians or "semicivilized."

It was at this point that his inner conflicts began to become apparent, paralleling his obvious inability to conform to the expectations of his fellow Englishmen. He was never happier than when in Indian, Afghan, or Arabian disguise, assuming a fictitious identity and mingling with the Indian and Arabian peoples, yet he longed to be admired and accepted by the English reading public. Early in life he asserted, with some bravado, that for the strong man every region is his home, but later in life he confessed that he wished he belonged to some "English parish" that might admire his accomplishments and welcome him home. Ultimately, it seems, his loyalty was not to England but to the British Empire, or to the *idea* of the Empire in its noblest aspirations. He could not abide life among his fellow Britishers, in general, but he did make some lifelong friends, attesting to his capacity for loyalty to a select few. He greatly admired many Eastern values and life-styles, especially in matters of relations between the sexes, and he likened Victorian morality to a cage of unhealthy ignorance and oppression. He sincerely felt that England sorely needed the sexual wisdom and knowledge of the East, which did little to recommend him to the proper Victorians; yet he described many of the legal and criminal practices of the Indians, especially as regards the power of the husband over the wife, as barbaric. He praised the Arabian spirit of independence, as shown in Arab resistance to Turkish domination, yet condemned that same spirit, in later years, when the Arabs and Egyptians refused to submit to British rule. And while stressing his belief in the white

Europeans' right to rule the world,[18] he preferred the Moslem religion to all others and was extremely sarcastic regarding Christian missionary efforts at conversion.

These inconsistencies in dealing with Eastern cultures stem from other, more personal, factions at war within him. Burton presented himself to the world both as a man of action and as a scholar, as a learned linguist and as a rough-neck brawler and libertine whose persona, as narrator in his travel books, was that of the confident conqueror of cultures, peoples, and hostile regions of the world. Yet in his secret soul he was a sensitive artist, a poet, and lifelong friend of Swinburne. Publicly Burton was a master of the arts of boxing, horsemanship, and swordsmanship; he published a book on the proper use of the bayonet (later adopted by the German and British military), advocated the use of the "dum-dum" bullet, and advised harsh punishments for maintaining both military and civil discipline; yet three of his chief idols were Cardinal Newman, Disraeli, and Lord Byron. And in Disraeli and Byron he saw embodiments of his own aspirations: they were both men of action and successful men of letters. Burton's description of Disraeli, in which he likened him to Byron, could apply equally well to himself: both his two idols had "that exceeding sensitiveness, that womanly (not effeminate) softness of heart which finds safety in self-concealment from the coarse, hard, and cruel world that girds it."[19] Burton took infinite pains to hide what he felt to be the poetic or "womanly" side of his nature, but it emerged when he published, anonymously, his efforts at poetry.

So, in sum, what do we find in Burton and his books on the East? We find a man whose writings on India are rich in colorful detail, personal anecdotes, history, geography, and learned discourses on languages and customs, along with prejudice, humor, sarcasm, and sometimes disenchantment. He was essentially a romantic who sought a world of exotic beauty, freedom, excitement, and sensuous fulfillment in the Orient, whereas he often found, as he describes in his first encounter with Bombay, a real world of poverty and disease, rats and congestion, and the stench of Hindu funeral burning-grounds. He had trouble forgiving India her imperfections, and he also berates the Empire for its failing, through ignorance and social clumsiness, to live up to its promise. He lavishes loving detail in describing the joys of his adventures among the Orientals, while hoping that his books will earn him respect from scholars and an admiring British audience. He developed a love for Al-Islam—her culture and religion, which he defended from Western critics in his posthumous *The Jew, The Gypsy, and El-Islam*— while in *Pilgrimage* he reveals, on nearly every page, his assumption of British superiority in general and his own in particular. While relishing his associations with most Arabs, he is critical of the city-dwellers, and he writes most affectionately of the desert people, the Bedouins, whose character and way of life he greatly admired— especially the Arabian "kayf," which, while encouraging surrendering oneself completely to the sensuous enjoyment of the moment, to a kind of "animal existence," is yet in Burton's view a product of a highly intelligent society.

Perhaps, of all the commentators on Burton's divided vision of the East, Edward Said is most provocative in his interpretation of the way in which Burton's preference for Eastern life coexists with his commitment to the Empire. Said suggests (to reduce greatly a complex argument) that it was Burton's mastery, his deep knowledge of the Oriental culture as an intricate system of codes, beliefs, and practices, that provides his British dominance and control over his Oriental experiences. Burton's books are a "testimony to his victory" over the intricate "system of Oriental knowledge." This is in itself a form of imperialism: "To be a European in the Orient, and to be one knowledgeably, one must see and know the Orient as a domain to be ruled over by Europe." In this way, the voice of Burton the individualist and the voice of the British Empire are coalesced. [20]

We do not know if Burton would agree with this view—that his double vision became one through his masterful display of knowledge—but it is clear that he was fully aware of his divided nature and need for "coalescence." Later in life, during periods of serious illness and delirium in West Africa and Brazil, he felt acutely that he had been split into two persons. For many years he lived with the conviction that he had a dual nature, seeing with two different sets of eyes, perpetually at war within himself. So he was not surprised, when being fitted with eye-glasses, to discover that his eyes measured differently and required very different lenses. "I always told you that I was a dual man," he said to his wife, "and I believe that that particular mania when I was delirious is perfectly correct." [21]

It may be true that Burton's knowledge of the East gave him a sense of imperial dominance, but his knowledge and dominance of himself remained always incomplete. On the surface he was opinionated and dogmatic, but fundamentally he was never sure of who or what he really was, where he belonged, or what he believed. It is the dramatic tension arising from his contradictions, and his quest for wholeness, that give vitality and human interest to his writings on the Orient. The impact of the East was strong enough to bring into temporary prominence Burton's native imaginative sympathies and emotional sensibility. This strength is first evidenced in many passages in *Pilgrimage* and reemerges in his later writings on Moslem East Africa, his own later poetry dealing with Oriental subjects, his books of Eastern erotica, and his translations of *The Arabian Nights*. But in addition to stimulating his emotional and imaginative faculties, the East provided Burton with material to indulge his urge to live robustly, his love for adventure, his penchant for the curious and "anthropological," and his staunch support for British imperialism. It has been said that "Burton found everything he needed in the East, or rather, that he was able to turn everything he found in the East to his own use. He was temperamentally susceptible to the romantic charms which the West is prone to ascribe to the East and he fell in love with them; but he was practical and matter-of-fact enough to appreciate the dowry as well."[22]

Burton returned to his first love, but only after his long and at times unpleasant detour through darkest Africa and the wilds of the New World. He engaged in many dramatic adventures and wrote some good books; and he also became involved in bitter feuds and discrediting controversies, embarked on a fruitless search for gold in the Midian, and wrote some dull books. Yet never did he diminish his earliest and, in a sense, spurious fame as "the first European to have penetrated the holy cities of Islam." This exploit, the emphasis upon its hazards reinforcing European convictions about the ferocity of the Moslems, and "the strangeness, the incomprehensible otherness, of their shrines," seemed to have "ushered in a new period of western fascination with Arabs and things Arabic."[23] The fascination was already there, as we have seen, and Burton served to reinforce it. Also, his journey served to lift forever a certain darkness that had, for the Europeans at least, lain over Mecca for a thousand years. Mystery had been replaced by knowledge. Indeed, it has been remarked that Burton's success made it unnecessary, as it were, for any other European to risk the journey to Mohammed's birthplace. It had been done and described, once and for all.

Yet the romance remained, at least as regards the desert. For it was the vast deserts of Arabia, and its enduring nomads who had learned to be as tough and fierce as their homeland, that increasingly drew the fascinated attention of Europe and especially England. Burton had helped create the myth of the noble Bedouin, a myth not without a basis in fact, a myth that would grip the Western imagination and fuel the popular arts for decades to come: painting, literature, light opera, and later the movies were all to exploit the image of the romantic desert sheik. This mirage was to draw into Arabia "a succession of lusty adventurers anxious to fling aside western dress and even, when they could, western characteristics, in order to woo and win the admiration and what was even better, the acceptance of the peripatic Arab of the desert."[24]

Thus, whatever scholars may think of Burton as an anthropologist, or as a literary artist, his books on the East, and especially *Pilgrimage*, have had a permanent impact on the Western world's conception of the Orient, just as Richard Burton himself, as dramatized in his books, helped model our image of the nineteenth-century hero.

Notes and References

Preface

1. Fawn Brodie, *The Devil Drives: A Life of Sir Richard Burton* (New York, 1967), 16. Quote from Burton is found in the foreword to his translation of *The Carmina of Gaius Valerius Catullus* (London, 1894). *The Devil Drives*, along with Isabel Burton's *Life*, is my principal source for the facts (and a few judgments) regarding Burton's biography.

2. See Norman St. John-Stevas, *Obscenity and the Law* (London: Secker & Warburg, 1956), and Alec Craig, *The Banned Books of England* (London, 1937), 46.

3. *Academy*, 25 October 1890, 365.

Chapter One

1. Arthur Symons, *Dramatis Personae* (Indianapolis, 1923), 251; Dunraven, *Past Times and Pasttimes* (London, 1922), 1:178—cited in Brodie, *Devil Drives*, 15.

2. See Frank Harris, *Contemporary Portraits* (New York, 1920), 180–82; and *My Life and Times* (New York, 1963), 616–21.

3. Brodie, *Devil Drives*, 19.

4. Isabel Burton, *Life of Captain Sir Richard F. Burton* (London, 1893), 2:257.

5. Ibid., 1:21.

6. This account of Burton's early years in France and Italy is from ibid., 1:52–75.

7. Brodie, *Devil Drives*, 39.

8. The information pertaining to Burton's days at Oxford is found in ibid., 1:75–90; and in Brodie, *Devil Drives*, 40–46.

9. Burton, *Life*, 1:101–7.

10. *A Personal Narrative of a Pilgrimage to El-Medinah and Meccah* (1893; reprint, New York, 1964), 2:100.

11. Brodie, *Devil Drives*, 51.

12. *Falconry in the Valley of the Indus* (London, 1852), 99–100; cited by Brodie, *Devil Drives*, 63.

13. Burton, *Life*, 1:52–54.

14. *Pilgrimage*, 1:141.

15. Ibid., 1:2.

16. Brodie, *Devil Drives*, 88. Most of the material for Burton's experience in Mecca and Medina are taken from his *Pilgrimage*, though I

have borrowed some comments on that material from Fawn Brodie and Isabel Burton.

17. This account has been drawn from *First Footsteps in East Africa* (London, 1856).

18. Brodie, *Devil Drives*, 124.

19. Burton, *Life*, 221–44.

20. The courtship is fully discussed in W. H. Wilkins, *The Romance of Isabel Lady Burton* (New York: Dodd, Mead, 1897), and is cited frequently by Brodie, *Devil Drives*.

21. John Speke, *What Led to the Discovery of the Source of the Nile* (London: William Blackwood & Sons, 1863); and *Journal of the Discovery of the Source of the Nile* (London: William Blackwood & Sons, 1864); Burton, *The Nile Basin*, Part I (Part II by James McQueen) (London: Tinsley Bros., 1864).

22. Brodie, *Devil Drives*, 182.

23. Ibid., 226.

24. Burton, *Life*, 1:546–65; an account of the Damascus experience is also found in Isabel Burton, *The Inner Life of Syria*, 2 vols. (London: Henry S. King, 1876).

25. Brodie, *Devil Drives*, 328.

26. Ibid., 331.

Chapter Two

1. "Autobiography" in Burton, *Life*, 1:163.

2. *Goa and the Blue Mountains* (London, 1851), 347; *Sindh, and the Races that Inhabit the Valley of the Indus* (London, 1851), 244.

3. "Notes and Remarks on Dr. Dorn's Chrestomathy of the Pushtu or Affghan Language" and "A Grammar of the Jataki or Belohcki Dialect" were published in *Royal Asiatic Society Journal* (Bombay Branch) 3, no. 12 (January 1849):58–69, 84–125. "Brief Notes relative to the Division of Time, and Articles of Cultivation in Sind" and "Notes relative to the Population of Sind; and the Customs, Language, and Literature of the People" were published in *Bombay Government Records*, no. 17, n.s. pt. 2 (1855):613–36, 637–57.

4. The manuscript can be seen at the Royal Anthropological Institute in London, according to Brodie, *Devil Drives*, 68.

5. Burton's fifth book on India is entitled *Sind Revisited; With Notices of the Anglo-Indian Army; Railroads; Past, Present, and Future*, 2 vols. (London, 1877). This work is essentially a reprint of *Sindh and the Races that Inhabit the Valley of the Indus* with, as the title indicates, some updated comments on railroads and the army. It is not clear why Burton could not decide how the name of the Indian province was to be spelled. Of the

choices, Scinde, Sindh, and Sind, I will use the latter in my own commentary.

6. For contrasting descriptions of travel through the same terrain at about the same time, see Mrs. Colin Mackenzie, *Life in the Mission, the Camp, and the Zanana* (London, 1854). For evidence that Burton's jaunty, sardonic style and making fun of the civilized Englishman's sufferings in barbaric India were the mode of the day, see [J. W. Kaye], *Peregrine Pultuney, or Life in India* (London: J. Mortimer, 1844); G. F. Atkinson, *Curry and Rice (on Forty Plates)* (London: Day & Son, 1853); and Emily Eden, *Up the Country,* E. Thompson (Oxford, 1937). For an entertaining general discussion of these and other Britishers in India, see Michael Edwardes, *Bound to Exile: The Victorians in India* (New York, Praeger, 1970).

7. Regarding this predilection for classifying people into distinct groups all sharing identical traits, Burton might have been influenced by the Indian erotica he was reading. In the *Kama Sutra of Vatsayana,* for example, we find that the women of the Dravida country do *this,* the women of Vanavasi do *that,* the women of Avant do *something* different. It was useful to know, for instance, that "the women of Ganda have tender bodies, and speak sweetly"—apparently without exception.

8. *Scinde,* 2 vols. (London, 1851).

9. Burton, *Life,* 1:248–49. This sentiment will be echoed by Kipling, whose admiration for the Indian woman's attachment to her child contrasted sharply with his painful exile from his parents while attending school back in England. Ameera, in "Without Benefit of Clergy," surely speaks for Kipling and closely echoes Burton on this subject of mothers and children.

10. All references in this study are to *Sindh,* preface by H. T. Hamrick (Karachi, 1973).

11. In his preface to ibid. H. T. Hamrick says, "Is not the extract from the Sindhi compendium on the subject of matrimony utterly delightful?" and he emphasizes that chapter 7 is "even more important, both for its exposition of Sufism, which continues to be the very essence of Sindhi thought and attitude to life, and for the closely related system of Piri-Muridi, so characteristic of society in the Indus valley" (ix, x).

12. This passage also appears in Burton's "Autobiography" as reproduced in Burton, *Life,* 1:155. The autobiography includes many pages taken directly from *Falconry.*

13. See Byron Farwell, *Burton: A Biography of Sir Richard Francis Burton* (New York, 1963), 55: "Curiously enough, the book was never remaindered and nearly sixty years after its publication (and twenty years after Burton's death) it could still be procured from the successors of the publishers."

14. Burton, *Life*, 1:158. Of *Scinde, or the Unhappy Valley*, she says, "For all that my husband *said* of India, he talked exactly as Mr. Rudyard Kipling writes, and when I read him, I can hear Richard talking; hence I knew how true and to the point are his writings" (*Life*, 1:159).

15. Farwell, *Burton*, 54, 53.

16. H. T. Hamrick, in *Sindh*, viii. Fawn Brodie calls *Sindh* "a solid brilliant ethnological study" (*Devil Drives*, 73).

Chapter Three

1. All citations in this study are from the two-volume Memorial Edition of *Pilgrimage* (London, 1893; reprint, New York, 1964); hereafter cited as *Pilgrimage*.

2. See Martha Pike Conant, *The Oriental Tale in England in the Eighteenth Century* (New York: Octagon Books, 1966).

3. See chapter 1, "Victorian Interest in the Arab World," in Thomas J. Assad's *Three Victorian Travellers: Burton, Blunt, Doughty* (London, 1964) for a useful brief discussion. See also Amy Cruse, *The Victorians and their Reading* (Boston and New York: Houghton Mifflin, 1936).

4. Passages like this, according to Zahra Freeth and H. V. F. Winstone, show that "Burton, the sceptic of the West, had an instinctive understanding of the oriental mind and manner" (*Explorers of Arabia* [New York, 1978], 125).

5. Norman Penzer, *An Annotated Bibliography of Sir Richard Burton* (London, 1923), 7.

6. *First Footsteps in East Africa*, 38.

7. *First Footsteps in East Africa*, 118; and *Pilgrimage*, 2:93–94.

Chapter Four

1. See Gordon Waterfield's introduction to *First Footsteps in East Africa* (London, 1966). This edition is invaluable for its learned introduction, notes, reprintings of sections of Burton's letters, and Burton's government reports; it also includes appendixes containing documents excised from earlier editions. However, references in this study, unless otherwise indicated, are to the two-volume 1856 London edition published by Longman, Brown, Green, and Longman.

2. Ibid., 19–20.

3. Ibid., 2:83–84. The "artificial causes" probably refers to the widespread practice of genital excision, or clitorectomy.

4. Earlier Burton stated that of all foreigners the English were the most hated, since they were trying, with some success, to abolish slavery, and Harar was one of the main centers of the trade. Incidentally, several biographers, including Isabel Burton, mistakenly say that Burton entered Harar disguised as a Moslem, an error probably caused by some misleading

entries in his diaries. See Waterfield, introduction to *First Footsteps in East Africa*, 4.

5. Farwell, *Burton*, 120. Perhaps the peoples of Somaliland do not remember, but Burton's achievements are well recognized, and sometimes debated, by modern anthropologists, and by London's Colonial Office where, we are assured, Burton's book has been often cited in connection with the recent (1970s and 1980s) Ethiopian-Somali conflicts. See Waterfield, introduction to *First Footsteps in East Africa*, 32–33. I. M. Lewis, a modern anthropologist with an intimate knowledge of Somali culture, has written that *First Footsteps in East Africa* "remains the best general description of northern Somali society" (*A Pastoral Democracy* [London: Oxford University Press, 1961], 32). Waterfield quotes Sir Arnold Wilson, in his Fifth Burton Memorial Lecture to the Royal Asia Society (27 May 1937): "He had great sympathy with and understanding of the common people, but little sympathy with their rulers" (35).

6. Waterfield says that "those who have known Somalis have found that they make good soldiers and officers. They are full of curiosity and travel the world, accepting almost any job without feeling a sense of inferiority, perhaps because they believe that they are superior to everyone else" (introduction to *First Footsteps in East Africa*, 31–32).

7. Ibid., 503–04.

8. Caroline Oliver, "Richard Burton: The Africa Years," in *Africa and its Explorers*, ed. Robert I. Rotberg (Cambridge, Mass., 1970), 69–70.

9. *The Lake Regions of Central Africa*, 2 vols. (London, 1856).

10. In order to give a complete picture of this expedition, scholars are required to consult Speke's *What Led to the Discovery of the Nile and Journal of the Discovery of the Source of the Nile* as supplements to Burton's book.

11. The name of "Kazeh," which Burton applies to this important Arab town, was apparently a mistake: "Curiously, Burton, who always paid close attention to the names of places and had phenomenal grasp of languages, called the town Kazeh. After Burton and Speke, the next European to reach this place was Stanley, who in June 1871 arrived here on his search for Livingstone. But the town was then called Tabora—as it is today—and Stanley was unable to find anyone who had ever heard of 'Kazeh' " (see Farwell, *Burton*, 156).

12. Burton, for all his linguistic skill, could make mistakes. Farwell, *Burton*, 166, says that, in describing the great lake to the north, the local natives spoke of "the Nyanza, which curiously Burton thought to be the name of a lake (the word 'Nyanza' means 'lake')." Burton was rarely caught in such errors.

13. Waterfield, introduction to *First Footsteps in East Africa*, 39.

14. For a discussion of the "brilliance" of Burton's book, see Oliver, "Richard Burton," 85.

15. *Zanzibar: City, Island, and Coast,* 2 vols. (London, 1872).

Chapter Five

1. *Wanderings in West Africa,* 2 vols. (London, 1865).

2. *Two Trips to Gorilla Land,* 2 vols. (London, 1876), 2:318, 320; *Abeokuta and the Cameroons Mountains,* 2 vols. (London, 1863), 2:172; and Brodie, *Devil Drives,* 208.

3. *Abeokuta,* 1:43–44.

4. *Gorilla Land,* 1:217–18; see also "A Day Amongst the Fans," in *Selected Papers on Anthropology,* ed. N. M. Penzer. Burton will revise his estimate of the American Indians after his trip to America, as will be discussed at the end of this chapter.

5. Farwell, who points out that Isabel did develop "a decidedly jealous attitude toward her naked African sisters" (*Burton,* 211).

6. Farwell points out evidence in *A Mission to Gelele* to indicate that Burton was welcomed *back* by the king (*Burton,* 228). Brodie discovered a letter to Monckton Milnes, dated 31 May 1863, in which Burton described his illicit visit (Brodie, *Devil Drive,* 212).

7. *A Mission to Gelele,* 2 vols. (London, 1864).

8. Saul Bellow's *Henderson the Rain King* offers an interesting example of the influence of Burton and his books. Bellow's hero Henderson makes a number of references to Burton in the story, and it is obvious that Bellow, in depicting King Dahfu and the Wariri tribe, has taken details directly from Burton's King Gelele and the Dahomans. See Rodrigues, "Bellow's Africa," *American Literature* 43, no. 2 (May 1971):246.

9. Burton to Monckton Milnes; cited by Brodie, *Devil Drives,* 213.

10. *Lake Regions,* 2:329.

11. Brodie, *Devil Drives,* 150.

12. *Lake Regions,* 2:113–14.

13. Ibid., 323–24.

14. Brodie, *Devil Drives,* 210.

15. *Gorilla Land,* 1:251–52, and in "A Day Amongst the Fans," in *Selected Papers,* ed. Penzer, with slightly different wording.

16. *Lake Regions,* 2:324–25.

17. See Brodie, *Devil Drives,* 151: "Despite his perspicacity and detachment, there is, one must admit, a vindictiveness in Burton's account of African peoples that does not appear in his descriptions of other races. And here, one suspects, as with some kinds of hatred, an element of envy." Brodie sees envy of two kinds: of the African's capacity to enjoy idleness, and of his reputation for sexual prowess.

18. *Lake Regions,* 2:340–41.

19. Again, the Fans must be seen as contradicting Burton's notion that the more "negroid," the more savage.

20. *Lake Regions*, 2:378.

21. *City of Saints* (London, 1861).

22. See references earlier in this chapter to comparisons between the American Indian and the sadistic Fans of Africa; and *Gorilla Land*, 1:217–18.

23. *City of the Saints*, 523. Brodie, who wrote a book about the Mormon leader Joseph Smith, says of the various nineteenth-century commentators on the Mormons, "none wrote as sagacious and thorough a study as Burton." See Brodie, *Devil Drives*, 184–88.

Chapter Six

1. *Vikram and the Vampire* (1870; reprint, New York, 1969). The edition used here is a reprint of the Memorial Edition published in London in 1893, edited by Isabel Burton, who provided a preface; it includes thirty-eight illustrations by Ernest Geiset.

2. Brodie points out that Burton inserted in the first tale, "The Vampire's First Story," a highly personal message, a paragraph not in the original but created by Burton. It describes a man who married a woman exactly like Isabel—plump and a strict moralist who prided herself on her spirituality, but whom he loved, amazingly enough, notwithstanding. Brodie says, "This was the closest Burton would ever come to a personal declaration, in print, that somewhat to his surprise he loved his wife" (*Devil Drives*, 238).

3. *The Kasidah of Haji Abdu El-Yezdi, a Lay of the Higher Law Translated and Annotated by his Friend and Pupil F. B.* (London, 1880; reprint, New York, 1965).

4. *A Plain and Literal Translation of the Arabian Nights' Entertainment*, 10 vols. (London, 1885).

5. Ibid., translator's foreword, 1:ix.

6. Ibid., 1:xvii.

7. While Scheherazade is probably the most familiar spelling of the young woman's name, Burton preferred Sharazad, and Payne gave it as Shehrzad.

8. See *Nights*, 10:173–74; and introduction to *The Portable Arabian Nights*, ed. Joseph Campbell (New York, 1952).

9. See Campbell's introduction (in ibid.) for a discussion of the relations between *The Arabian Nights* and European literature.

10. See Judith Grossman, "Infidelity and Fiction: The Discovery of Women's Subjectivity in *Arabian Nights*," *Georgia Review* 34, no. 1 (Spring 1980):113–26.

11. Campbell, ed., *Portable Arabian Nights*, 42–43.

12. For a discussion of the relative merits of *The Arabian Nights* translations, in which Henry Torrens emerges as the winner, see Duncan B. Macdonald, "On Translating the *Arabian Nights*," *Nation* 71 (30 August–6 September 1900):167–68.

13. Ibid., 168.

14. Cited by Brodie, *Devil Drives*, 341.

15. Penzer, *Annotated Bibliography*, 319.

16. Campbell, ed., *Portable Arabian Nights*, 31–32.

17. See Brodie's admirable summary of the "Burton-Payne Controversy" (to which I am indebted in this commentary) in *Devil Drives*, 341–43.

18. Ameen Rihani, "The Coming of the *Arabian Nights*," *Bookman* (London) 35 (June 1912):503–8.

19. Macdonald, "On Translating," 186.

20. Kenneth Walker gives a detailed discussion of Burton's motives in translating *The Arabian Nights*. See his introduction to *Love, War and Fancy. The Customs and Manners of the East from Writings on the Arabian Nights by Sir Richard Burton*, ed. Kenneth Walker (London, 1964).

21. Isabel Burton, in the appendix to her *Life*, has reprinted twenty-four reviews of various volumes of *The Arabian Nights* that appeared during 1885–86 in English and Canadian newspapers. Some of them are brief, some are long and scholarly, but all of them are full of praise. She also reproduced letters from ten scholars commending Burton and his work. See *Life*, 2:617–28.

22. Ibid., 2:442.

Chapter Seven

1. See Wayland Young, *Eros Denied* (London, 1967), 197.

2. *Supplemental Nights to the Book of the Thousand Nights*, 6 vols. (London, 1886–88), 7:404, 439.

3. Foreword to *Arabian Nights*, 1:xix.

4. *Supplemental Nights*, 7:438; *Arabian Nights*, 10:2000.

5. *Supplemental Nights*, 5:42.

6. I will not be discussing this third form in which Burton's erotic writings appeared, since they are largely reprints or "borrowings." Two notable examples are included in the bibliography: *The Erotic Traveler* and *The Sotadic Zone*.

7. Farwell, *Burton*, 363. Biographers differ on this matter. Brodie says that the book was published in 1873, that it was privately printed but "after printing four or six copies the printers became alarmed and refused to print more for fear of prosecution" (*Devil Drives*, 372).

8. *Ananga Ranga* (London, 1885; reprint, New York, 1964).

9. *The Kama Sutra of Vatsyayana* (New York, 1963).

10. K. M. Panikkar, introduction to ibid., 19–20.
11. Ibid., 19.
12. Ibid., 30.
13. Archer, preface to ibid., 17.
14. Francis Watson, "Must We Burn Vatsyayana?" *Encounter*, March 1964, 70; cited by Brodie, *Devil Drives*, 297.
15. *Il Pentamerone*, intro. E. R. Vincent (London, n.d.).
16. Ibid., 6.
17. See Brodie for an interesting exchange of letters by Isabel, Smithers, and Burton regarding the hazards of acknowledging authorship (*Devil Drives*, 319–20).
18. Thomas Wright, *The Life of Sir Richard Burton* 2 vols. (New York, 1906), 2:217.
19. Isabel was not the only reader to have the curious notion that the *Garden* had a homosexual bias. G. Legman, among others, refers to the "homosexually oriented edition or 'translation' of the *Perfumed Garden of Al-Nefzawi*" (*The Horn Book: Studies in Erotic Folklore and Bibliography* [New York: University Books, 1964], 42).
20. While Burton's original translation from the French retained the French spelling, Cheikh Nefzaoui, more recent editions have seen fit to anglicize the spelling—Shaykh Nefzawi—which is the case with the edition used in this study: *The Perfumed Garden of the Shaykh Nefzawi*, ed. Alan Hull Walton (New York, 1964).
21. Walton, introduction to ibid., 28.
22. *Arabian Nights*, 5:76.
23. Walton, introduction to *The Perfumed Garden*. In addition to Havelock Ellis, Walton sees strong evidence of Burton's influence in Malinowski's *The Sexual Life of Savages* (London, 1932); Alfred Kinsey's *Sexual Behavior in the Human Male* (1948); Van de Velde's *Ideal Marriage* (1929); Eustace Chesser's *Love Without Fear* (1940); and the various works of Eberhard and Phyllis Kronhausen.
24. For these examples of Burton's influence, I am indebted to Walton's introduction to the *Perfumed Garden*.
25. Ibid., 54–55.

Chapter Eight

1. J. S. Cotton, obituary, *Academy*, 25 October 1890, 365.
2. Brodie, *Devil Drives*, 333, who, after writing her book on Burton, produced a study of Joseph Smith, the Mormon leader.
3. Cotton, obituary, 365.
4. Brodie, *Devil Drives*, 334.
5. See notes to the previous chapter regarding the twentieth-century scholars.

6. Farwell, *Burton*, 54.

7. Brodie, *Devil Drives*, 73.

8. Hamrick, introduction to *Sindh*, viii.

9. Cited by Assad, *Three Victorian Travelers*, who does not give the publication.

10. Symons, "A Neglected Genius: Sir Richard Burton," in *Dramatis Personae*, 242, 245.

11. Stephen Ely Tabachnick, *T. E. Lawrence* (Boston: Twayne, 1978), 31–32.

12. *The Lake Regions of Central Africa*, ed. Alan Moorehead, 2 vols. (New York, 1961), xi. Moorehead is the author of the excellently written *The White Nile* (1960) and *The Blue Nile* (1962).

13. Seton Dearden, *The Arabian Knight: A Study of Sir Richard Burton*, rev. ed. (London, 1953), 9–10: "As a student and recorder of human habit, as a tireless collector of facts, Burton is unsurpassable. He is less gifted in his comprehension of human nature and particularly oriental psychology, that subtle, sliding spirit of the Semite so deftly evoked by Doughty or by Palgrave. . . . This failure to understand character, this indifference to the feelings and opinions in others, are the chief defects in Burton's character and writings. . . . he did not understand Arabs."

14. Achmed Abdullah and T. Compton Pakenham, *Dreamers of Empire* (Freeport, N.Y., 1968), 57–58. Regarding "the riddle of the Arab": "Many have tried to solve it. Only one has succeeded." When one wants to solve that riddle, it requires more than minute observation and academic digging; it requires "the feeling, the instinctive, almost psychic reaction and perception. And there was one man, England's greatest traveler and linguist, who had this quality. Sir Richard Burton. Who else? . . . He saw eye to eye with the Arab." See also Freeth and Winstone, *Explorers of Arabia*.

15. Assad, *Three Victorian Travellers*, x.

16. Michael Voss, "Dangerous Guides: English Writers and the Desert," *New Middle East*, no. 9 (June 1969):39. Voss also states that Burton's "*Pilgrimage* added practically nothing to the European knowledge of Arabia" (38).

17. Edward Said, *Orientalism* (New York, 1978), 194–95.

18. Burton's views on British imperialism are implicit in his early writings. He is more explicit, even vehement, in the preface to the book that follows *Pilgrimage: First Footsteps in East Africa*.

19. *Lord Beaconsfield: A Sketch by Captain Richard Burton* (London, 1881), 7, as cited by Brodie, *Devil Drives*, 276.

20. Said, *Orientalism*, 196–97.

21. Burton, *Life*, 2:268.

22. Assad, *Three Victorian Travellers*, 52.

23. Peter Brent, *Far Arabia: Explorers of the Myth* (London, 1977), 119.

24. Ibid., 120.

Selected Bibliography

PRIMARY WORKS

1. Travel and Exploration

Abeokuta and the Cameroons Mountains: An Exploration. 2 vols. London: Tinsley Brothers, 1863.

The City of the Saints and Across the Rocky Mountains to California. London: Longman, Green, & Roberts, 1861.

Etruscan Bologna: A Study. London: Smith, Elder, & Co., 1876.

Falconry in the Valley of the Indus. London: J. Van Voorst, 1852.

First Footsteps in East Africa: or, An Exploration of Harar. 2 vols. London: Longman, Brown, Green, & Longmans, 1856. Reprint. London: Routledge & Kegan Paul, 1966.

Goa and the Blue Mountains; or, Six Months of Sick Leave. London: R. Bentley, 1851.

The Gold Mines of Midian and the Ruined Midianite Cities: A Fortnight's Tour in Northwestern Arabia. London: C. K. Paul & Co., 1878.

The Highlands of Brazil. 2 vols. London: Tinsley Brothers, 1869.

The Jew, the Gypsy, and El Islam. Edited with preface and brief notes, by W. H. Wilkins. Chicago: H. S. Stone & Co., 1898.

The Lake Regions of Central Africa: A Picture of Exploration. 2 vols. Longman, Green, Longman, & Roberts, 1856. Reprint. Edited by Alan Moorehead. New York: Horizon Press, 1961.

The Land of Midian (Revisited). 2 vols. London: C. K. Paul & Co., 1879.

Letters from the Battle-fields of Paraguay. London: Tinsley Brothers, 1870.

A Mission to Gelele, King of Dahome, With Notices of the So-Called "Amazons," the Grand Customs, the Yearly Customs, the Human Sacrifices, the Present State of the Slave Trade, and the Negro's Place in Nature. 2 vols. London: Tinsley Brothers, 1864.

Personal Narrative of a Pilgrimage to El-Medinah and Meccah. 3 vols. London: Longman, Brown, Green, & Longmans. Reprint. Memorial Edition. Introduction by Isabel Burton. 2 vols. London: Tylston & Edwards, 1893; New York: Dover Publications, 1964.

Scinde; or, The Unhappy Valley. 2 vols. London: R. Bentley, 1851.

Sindh, and the Races that Inhabit the Valley of the Indus; With Notices of the Topography and History of the Province. London: W. H. Allen, 1851.

Reprint. Preface by H. T. Hamrick. Karachi: Oxford University Press, 1973.

Sind Revisited; With Notices of the Anglo-Indian Army; Railroads; Past, Present, and Future, etc. 2 vols. London: R. Bentley & Son, 1877.

To the Gold Coast for Gold: A Personal Narrative by Richard F. Burton and Verney Lovett Cameron. 2 vols. London: Chatto & Windus, 1883.

Two Trips to Gorilla Land and the Cataracts of the Congo. 2 vols. London: S. Low, Marston, Low, & Searle, 1876.

Ultima Thule; or A Summer in Iceland. 2 vols. London: W. P. Nimmo, 1875.

Unexplored Syria, Visits to The Libanus, The Tulul el Safa, The Anti-Libanus, The Northern Libanus, and the 'Alah. 2 vols. London: Tinsley Brothers, 1871. with Charles F. Tyrwhitt-Drake.

Wanderings in Three Continents. Edited, with preface and brief notes, by W. H. Wilkins. London: Hutchinson & Co., 1901.

Wanderings in West Africa, From Liverpool to Fernando Po. 2 vols. London: Tinsley Brothers, 1863.

Zanzibar: City, Island, and Coast. 2 vols. London: Tinsley Brothers, 1872.

2. Translations

Ananga Ranga; (Stage of the Bodiless One) or, The Hindu Art of Love (Ars Amoris Indica): Translated from the Sanskrit, and Annotated by A. F. F. & B. F. R. London: Kama Shastra Society, 1885. Reprint. New York: Medical Press, 1964.

A Plain and Literal Translation of the Arabian Nights' Entertainments, Now Entitled The Book of The Thousand Nights and a Night: With Introduction, Explanatory Notes on the Manners and Customs of Moslem Men and a Terminal Essay upon the History of the Nights. 10 vols. London: Kama-Shastra Society, 1885.

Camoens, The Lyricks: Englished by Richard F. Burton. London: B. Quaritch, 1884.

The Carmina of Gaius Valerius Catullus, Now first completely Englished into Verse and Prose, the Metrical Part by Capt. Sir Richard F. Burton . . . and the Prose Portion, Introduction, and Notes Explanatory and Illustrative by Leonard C. Smithers. London, 1894.

Il Pentamerone; or, the Tale of Tales: Being a Translation by the Late Sir Richard Burton. 1893. Reprint. Introduction by E. R. Vincent. London: Spring Books, n.d.

The Kama Sutra of Vatsyayana . . . With a Preface and Introduction. London: Kama Shastra Society, 1883. Reprint. Edited, with preface, by W. G. Archer; introduction by K. M. Panikkar. New York: G. P. Putnam's Sons, 1963.

*The Kasidah of Haji Abdu El-Yezdi, a Lay of the Higher Law Translated and
    Annotated by his Friend and Pupil F. B.* London: Privately printed,
    1880. Reprint. New York: Citadel Press, 1965. Burton is author of
    both the poem and its annotations.

Os Lusiads (The Lusiads): Englished by Richard Francis Burton. Edited by
    Isabel Burton. 2 vols. London: B. Quaritch, 1880.

*The Perfumed Garden of the Cheikh Nefzaoui, A Manual of Arabian Erotology
    (XVI Century).* London: Kama Shastra Society, 1886. Reprint. In-
    troduction and additional notes by Alan Hull Walton. New York:
    G. P. Putnam's Sons, 1964.

*Priapeia or the Sportive Epigrams of divers Poets on Priapus: The Latin Text now
    for the first time Englished in Verse and Prose (the Metrical Version by
    "Outidanos") with Introduction, Notes Explanatory and Illustrative, and
    Excursus, by "Neaniskos."* London, 1890. Burton is responsible for the
    translation into poetry; the remainder of the volume is believed to
    be the work of his collaborator, Leonard Smithers.

*Supplemental Nights to the Book of the Thousand Nights and a Night With
    Notes Anthropological and Explanatory by Richard F. Burton.* 6 vols.
    London: Kama Shastra Society, 1886–88.

*Vikram and the Vampire, or Tales of Hindu Devilry: Adapted by Richard F.
    Burton.* London: Longmans, Green, & Co., 1870. Reprint. Memorial
    Edition. Preface by Isabel Burton. London, 1893; New York: Dover
    Publications, 1969.

3. Other Writings and Special Editions

Camoens: His Life and his Lusiads. London: B. Quaritch, 1881.

The Erotic Traveler. Edited by Edward Leigh. New York: G. P. Putnam's
    Sons, 1967. Passages of erotic subject matter taken from Burton's
    travel books and arranged, with some explanatory commentary, by
    the editor.

*The Kasidah of Haji Abdu El-Yezdi, A Lay of the Higher Law. Translated
    and Annotated by his Friend and Pupil F. B.* London: Privately printed,
    1880; Reprint. New York: Citadel Press, 1965.

*Love, War and Fancy, the Social and Sexual Customs of the East from the
    Writings on the Arabian Nights by Sir Richard Burton.* Edited, with
    introduction, by Kenneth Walker. London: W. Kimber, 1964.

Selected Papers on Anthropology, Travel and Exploration. Edited, with intro-
    duction and occasional notes, by N. M. Penzer. New York: R. M.
    McBride & Co., 1924.

The Sotadic Zone. Boston: Longwood Press, 1977. Reprint of an edition
    first printed privately by Panurge, (New York, n.d.) and containing
    passages from Burton's "Terminal Essay" of his original edition of
    the *Arabian Nights* dealing exclusively with pederasty.

SECONDARY SOURCES

1. Bibliography
Penzer, Norman A. *An Annotated Bibliography of Sir Richard Francis Burton.* London: A. M. Philpot, 1923.

2. Books and Parts of Books
Abdullah, Achmed, and **Pakenham, T. Compton.** *Dreamers of Empire.* 1929. Reprint. Freeport, N.Y.: Books for Library Press, 1968. Survey of the early explorers of the Middle East. Looks favorably on Burton and his books, claiming that of all the British writers about Arabia, he understood most clearly the people and their culture.
Assad, Thomas J. *Three Victorian Travellers: Burton, Blunt, Doughty.* London: Routledge & Kegan Paul, 1964. Perceptive evaluation of the three travelers as observers of the culture and peoples of the Middle East. Sees Burton as one of the more accurate commentators on Arabia and Arabian character.
Brent, Peter. *Far Arabia, Explorers of the Myth.* London: Weidenfeld & Nicholson, 1977, pp. 101–21. Evaluates Burton, among others, as a contributor to the creation of the "myth" of Arabia. Sees Burton as important in the romanticizing of the desert Arab, especially the Bedouin.
Brodie, Fawn. *The Devil Drives: A Life of Sir Richard Burton.* New York: W. W. Norton & Co., 1967. One of the more recent, and probably the best, of the biographies of Burton. Written with clarity, grace, and humor, the work is fully documented, thorough in its coverage, balanced and judicious in its evaluations.
Burton, Isabel. *Life of Captain Sir Richard F. Burton.* 2 vols. London: Chapman & Hall, 1893. The principal source of information about Burton's life. Not reliable in its value judgments, but contains indispensable materials: letters to and from Burton, sections of his otherwise unpublished autobiography and diary, and records of Burton's conversations, problems he had with publishers regarding the contents of some of his books — and with his wife regarding the same. This work has been drawn upon extensively by all subsequent biographers.
Campbell, Joseph. Introduction to *The Portable Arabian Nights.* New York: Viking Press, 1952. In introducing selections from Payne's translations, Campbell offers useful information about *The Arabian Nights* in general; downgrades Burton's achievement, echoing those critics who saw Burton's translation as largely a plagiarism of Payne's.

Craig, Alec. *The Banned Books of England.* London: Allen & Unwin, 1962. Useful in understanding the risks Burton was taking in publishing his works of "erotica." Documents the activities of such organizations as the society for the Suppression of Vice in encouraging the prosecution of writers and publishers during the Victorian era.

Dearden, Seton. *The Arabian Knight: A Study of Sir Richard Burton.* Rev. ed. London: Arthur Barker, 1953. Praises Burton as a collector of facts but asserts that his "failure to understand character," his "indifference to the feelings and opinions of others," are the chief defects in Burton's character and writings.

Downey, Fairfax. *Burton, Arabian Nights Adventurer.* New York: Scribner's Sons, 1931. One of many popularized biographies of Burton, emphasizing his years in the Middle East. Superseded by the biographies by Byron Farwell and Fawn Brodie.

Edwardes, Allen. *Death Rides a Camel.* New York: Julian Press, 1963. Another popular biography of Burton, claiming to be an exposé and concentrating on the more sensational aspects of Burton's career. Interesting primarily as an example of the kind of sensation-mongering which Burton's writings attracted.

Farwell, Byron. *Burton: A Biography of Sir Richard Francis Burton.* New York: Holt, Rinehart, & Winston, 1963. An interesting and well-written study of Burton, apparently based on careful scholarship but lacking in footnotes or other forms of documentation.

Freeth, Zahra, and **Winstone, H. V. F.** *Explorers of Arabia.* New York: Holmes & Meier, 1978. Gives an admiring account of Burton's writings on Arabia, believing him to have an accurate insight into and understanding of Arabian culture.

Hamrick, H. T. Preface to *Sindh and the Races that Inhabit the Valley of the Indus,* London: Oxford University Press, 1973. A scholarly discussion of Burton's contribution to modern knowledge of the cultures of the province of Sind.

Harris, Frank. *Contemporary Portraits.* New York: Mitchell Kennerley, 1915, pp. 180–82.

———. *My Life and Loves.* New York: Grove Press, 1963, pp. 616–21. Lively commentary on Burton's character and writings by an admirer who felt that Burton's work did not receive the praise which it deserved.

Kiernan, R. H. *The Unveiling of Arabia.* 1937. Reprint. New York: AMS Press, 1975. Useful for general information about the various European explorers of Arabia but does not shed much light on Burton's writings.

Moorehead, Alan. *The Blue Nile.* New York: Harper & Row, 1962.

————. *The White Nile.* Harper & Row, 1960. Fascinating accounts of the persons and historical events associated with the explorations of the two branches of the Nile River, with brief accounts of Burton's activities. Of more importance to this study is the introduction to Moorehead's edition of *The Lake Regions of Central Africa* in which Moorehead expresses high praise for Burton both as an explorer and a writer.

Oliver, Caroline. "Richard Burton: The African Years." In *Africa and its Explorers,* ed. Robert I. Rotberg. Cambridge: Harvard University Press, 1970. A brief summary of Burton's travels which praises the "brilliance" of his contributions to anthropological knowledge of Africa but insists that Burton's writings are seriously marred by his racial prejudice.

Panikkar, K. M. Introduction to *The Kama Sutra of Vatsyayana.* New York: Putnam's Sons, 1963. Informative disscussion of *The Kama Sutra* in terms of Indian manners, morals, and values, intended to explain to Western readers the place of the work in Indian culture. Especially interesting regarding the religious dimension of *The Kama Sutra.*

Said, Edward. *Orientalism.* New York: Pantheon Books, 1978. Includes a provocative analysis of Burton's "dualism" — the tension between his sympathetic identification with Eastern culture and values and his conception of himself as an agent of British imperialism. Sees Burton's knowledge and mastery of Eastern languages and cultures as a form of "imperialism." A stimulating if controversial commentary.

Symons, Arthur. "A Neglected Genius: Sir Richard Burton." In *Dramatis Personae.* Indianapolis: Bobbs-Merrill Co., 1923. A spirited if somewhat partial defense of Burton's character — his personality and social manners — as well as of his writings and contributions to knowledge of Eastern peoples. Praises Burton's literary style and feels that his "genius" had been shamefully ignored, or undervalued, by British authorities.

Walker, Kenneth. Introduction to *Love, War and Fancy: The Social and Sexual Customs of the East.* London: W. Kimber, 1964. Selection of Burton's writings. A useful discussion that stresses the author's "motives" in writing about the East and in translating *The Arabian Nights,* especially Burton's desire to educate the British public in general and the Foreign Office in particular, with the intention of making British foreign policy more effective.

Walton, Alan Hull. Introduction to *The Perfumed Garden of the Shaykh Nefzawi.* New York: Putnam's Sons, 1963. Useful survey of the main themes featured in the Arabic manual of love.

Waterfield, Gordon. Introduction to *First Footsteps in East Africa.* London: Routledge & K. Paul, 1966. Drawing extensively on Burton's letters

and government reports found in British government archives, Waterfield provides information about the conditions of Burton's writing
of *First Footsteps*. Places the book in the context of Burton's other
writings.

Wright, Thomas. *The Life of Sir Richard Burton.* 2 vols. New York: Putnam's Sons, 1906. This work has been superseded by the biographies
by Farwell and Brodie. Interesting primarily for its generally negative
view of Burton. Wright, who was later to write an admiring biography of John Payne, admitted that he wrote the Burton biography
in order to discredit him and to "prove" that Burton had stolen his
translations of *The Arabian Nights* from those of Payne.

Young, Wayland. *Eros Denied.* New York: Grove Press, 1964. An interesting discussion of, among other things, the Victorian attitudes
toward sexuality. Gives good background to Burton's courageous
efforts to publish his books on Eastern art of love.

3. Articles

Baker, F. Grenfell. "Sir Richard Burton as I Knew Him." *Cornhill Mag-
azine,* no. 304 (October 1921):411–23. An account of Burton's personality and character by the man who was Burton's personal physician
during Burton's later years.

Burton, Isabel. "Sir Richard Burton: an Explanation and a Defence." *New
Review* (November 1892):572–78. Isabel's attempt to explain and to
justify her burning of her husband's papers after his death.

Cannon, J. S. "Obituary." *Academy,* 25 October 1890, 365. Primarily a
eulogy, stressing Burton's great achievements, quite accurately, and
avoiding negative commentary.

Dupee, F. W. "Sir Richard and Ruffian Dick." *New York Review of Books,*
16 April 1964, 3ff. A review-essay of Byron Farwell's *Burton* (1963)
in which Dupee expresses most of the standard views of the deficencies
in Burton's character.

Foss, Michael. "Dangerous Guides: English Writers and the Desert." *New
Middle East,* no. 9 (June 1969): 38-42. A sharp criticism of several
Victorian travel-writers, including Burton, in which Foss asserts that
all those writers, under the influence of an *Arabian Nights'* romanticism, wrote a species of "fiction" rather than authentic accounts of
the desert Arab.

Macdonald, Duncan B. "On Translating the Arabian Nights." *Nation* 71
(30 August–6 September 1900): 167–68, 185–86. An appraisal of
the best-known translations of *The Arabian Nights,* including Burton's, by a notable scholar (the author of the entry on "Alf Laila Wa-
Laila [Thousand nights and a night]" in the *Encyclopedia of Islam,*

supp. 1) in which he points out the strengths and weaknesses of each translation, indicating his preference for that of Henry Torrens.

Rihani, Ameen. "The coming of the *Arabian Nights.*" *Bookman* (London) 35 (June 1912):503–8. The Arabian scholar assesses and compares the translations of Payne and Burton, concluding that both fail to convey the lyricism of the original, that the Arabic rhythm cannot be reproduced in English.

Index